EARL FITZWILLIAM'S
TREASURE ISLAND

EARL FITZWILLIAM'S TREASURE ISLAND

The Mystery of the Cheerio Trail

STEPHEN COOPER & JOHN MOORHOUSE

ISBN-13: 9781522961420
ISBN-10: 1522961429

'Dr. Livesey, and the rest of these gentlemen having asked me to write down the whole particulars about Treasure Island, from the beginning to the end, keeping nothing back but the bearings of the island, and that only because there is still treasure not yet lifted.'

Jim Hawkins, in *Treasure Island*
by Robert Louis Stevenson.

'There comes a time in every rightly constructed boy's life when he has a raging desire to go somewhere and dig for buried treasure.'

Mark Twain, cited in *The Book of Buried Treasure*
by Ralph D. Paines

CONTENTS

Introduction · ix
Acknowledgements · xi

Chapter 1   Treasure Island · 1
Chapter 2   The Earl and the Admiral · · · · · · · · · · · · · · · · · · 8
Chapter 3   The Voyage· 15
Chapter 4   The Explosion· 25
Chapter 5   Rumours and Spin · 34
Chapter 6   A Second Expedition? · 41
Chapter 7   The Cheerio Trail · 51
Chapter 8   The Mystery Solved? · 60

Sources · 65
Illustrations · 67

INTRODUCTION

❜The Cheerio Trail' was a story told in the village of Wentworth in South Yorkshire in the middle of the 20th century. As a way of avoiding questions about a mysterious expedition to the South Pacific, those who had accompanied the 7th Earl Fitzwilliam (1872-1943) and might have been expected to know the truth of it, would cut the conversation short and walk away, saying 'Cheerio for now'; and they never came back to tell the tale.

Social and economic change has altered everyone's way of life since then; and dynastic accident brought about a dramatic reversal of fortune for the Fitzwilliam family. The Earldom became extinct in 1979. The Earl's seat in Coolattin, County Wicklow, has become a golf club.[1] His London home in Mayfair is now the Italian Embassy. His palatial mansion, Wentworth Woodhouse – which in its heyday was Downton Abbey writ large – has suffered greatly from mining subsidence and is now for sale. Yet the mystery of 'The Cheerio Trail' remains unsolved.

In her brilliant first book, *Black Diamonds* (Viking, 2007; Penguin, 2008) Catherine Bailey described the obsessive secrecy of successive members of the Fitzwilliam family. There were scandals about the mysterious birth of the 7th Earl in a log cabin in Canada in 1872; his Aunt Alice's theft of the family's valuables in 1902; and the 8th Earl's affair with Kathleen Kennedy in 1948.

---

1 www.coollattingolfclub.com.

Moreover, various attempts to keep these matters secret culminated in the burning, in 1972, of virtually all the family papers.[2]

Bailey gave us convincing answers to most of the questions she posed; but she did not discuss 'The Cheerio Trail'. This book reveals the true story of what happened in 1904-5; and why the truth was kept hidden for so long.

---

2 Bailey, xxii; 22, 57, 61; chapter 34, 437.

ACKNOWLEDGEMENTS

We would not have written this book unless John had conceived the idea. We both greatly enjoyed *The Big House and the Little Village* by Roy Young and *Black Diamonds* by Catherine Bailey and have made much use of them. Professor Melvyn Jones pointed us to the two principal sources, donated the map of the voyage of the *Véronique*, helped to correct the original typescript and offered many helpful suggestions. The photograph of Earl Fitzwilliam on Cocos Island is reproduced by kind permission of Roy Young and Wentworth Garden Centre, the publishers of *The Big House and the Little Village*. The photographs of the Earl in 1905, Admiral Palliser, the *Véronique*, the little dog, and the cartoon are taken from George Eustace Cooke-Yarborough's Journal, a copy of which is in Doncaster Archives, and is reproduced with their kind permission and with that of the copyright owner, Mr Anthony Cooke-Yarborough. Quotations from British newspapers are included by permission of The British Newspaper Archive. At a late stage in publication Anthony also kindly lent us his grandfather Eustace's photograph album, from which other photos were taken.

Stephen Cooper & John Moorhouse, January 2016.

Chapter 1

TREASURE ISLAND

Cocos Island lies 300 miles off the coast of Costa Rica, on the western or Pacific side. It is volcanic in origin, about four miles long and three miles wide. It is not to be confused with the Cocos (Keeling) Islands, which are in the middle of the Indian Ocean and belong to Australia, nor with Cocos Island, which is in the Bay of Bengal. Surrounded by deep water, the Island is nowadays admired by divers for its Hammerhead sharks, rays, dolphins and other marine animals.[3]

There were three main legends concerning buried treasure on Cocos Island. One started with a woman named Mary Welsh, who claimed that 350 tons of gold raided from Spanish galleons had been buried there. She had been a member of a pirate crew led by Captain Bennett Graham and was transported to Australia for her crimes; but she had a chart showing where Graham's treasure was supposed to be hidden; and on her release she made her way to the Island again with an expedition which, alas, found nothing. There was another story concerning the Portuguese pirate Benito Bonito, who was executed, but not before burying his treasure. Lastly, there was the story of the 'Treasure of Lima.' This is sometimes thought to have been synonymous with the 'treasure of the Incas', although the last Inca ruler had been murdered by the Spaniards

---

3 Mariella Frostrup had a diving holiday there in 1997: *The Observer*, 16 February 1997.

in the 1570s. It is of course possible that all three traditions contained a grain of truth; and that there was (or is) more than one hoard on Cocos Island.[4]

The fabulous Treasure of Lima consisted of a vast reserve of gold and silver which the Spaniards had accumulated in their Peruvian capital, but were unable to bring home to Spain because of the wars of independence in Central and South America. In 1820, when the army of the Liberator José de San Martín was approaching Lima, the Spanish Viceroy is supposed to have entrusted the imperial treasure to a British trader, Captain William Thompson, so that he could convey it to a place of safety. Instead of doing that, Thompson and his crew killed the Viceroy's men and sailed to Cocos Island, where they buried their ill-gotten gains. Shortly afterwards, they were arrested by a Spanish warship and the whole crew (except Thompson and his first mate) were executed for piracy. In exchange for their lives, the two survivors promised to reveal where the treasure was hidden; but, once on the Island, they ran off into the jungle. To complicate matters, there are various stories as to how Thompson escaped and handed his secret down to other adventurers.

According to the best accounts, the treasure was hidden in a cave, somewhere near Chatham Bay, on the north-east corner of the Island; but various people claimed to have maps or 'Clues' as to its precise whereabouts. There were several expeditions in the mid-19th century, inspired by the claims of John Keating, who was supposed to have befriended Thompson. The first seems to have been undertaken in 1872, when the brig *Laura* set sail from San Francisco.[5] In the 1890s one Joseph Relf, who had served in the Royal Navy on the Pacific Station and subsequently became the first coastguard to be awarded the M.B.E, set off in search of the treasure. His party was said to have dug 'tremendous trenches' on Cocos Island, but all to no avail, because 'the tropical rain soon washed away all their work.'[6]

A report filed from British Columbia, which appeared in *the Edinburgh Evening News* on 8 August 1902, stated that the brigantine *Blakely* had recently arrived in the port of Victoria, with a group who had returned from a

---

4 For the early history see Hancock & Weston.

5 *Pall Mall Gazette*, 3 August 1872.

6 *Dundee Evening Telegraph*, 21 October 1938; *Dundee Courier* 28. August 1945 (obituary).

VAIN HUNT FOR TREASURE

The report went on to tell the reader that 'those on board say that they have had hard luck and they believe there is no treasure on the island.' Another report in 1904 confirmed the voyage of the *Blakely* and referred to several other attempts, including one led by a Captain James Brown of Rhode Island, U.S.A., though he subsequently reported that the treasure had been moved, as long ago as 1849, to an entirely different location.[7]

Enter Henry Palliser (1839 – 1907). His interest in Cocos Island had possibly been awakened by a letter received from a fellow Irishman, Patrick Fitzgerald. In 1882 he acquired a map of the Island, purporting to show the exact location of the hoard. We may wonder where the map came from; but historians tell us that many such maps have been made over time, indeed that 'if all [the] documents, charts and maps were laid side by side, they would blanket the island.'[8]

Palliser first visited Cocos Island for himself in 1897 when he was stationed on the Royal Navy's Pacific Station. While on board H.M.S. *Impérieuse*, he made a landing on the island while its Governor, Herr August Gissler, was temporarily away. Without obtaining permission from anyone, he sent several platoons of marines ashore with shovels, picks and large quantities of dynamite. Ignoring the protests of Frau Gissler, they excavated, blasted large holes in several places, and vandalised the Island for several days, but found nothing. Great Britain may once have been famous for 'gunboat diplomacy' but with hindsight this seems more like piracy and, even in 1897, Palliser was severely reprimanded by his superiors, though he was also promoted soon afterwards.[9]

In 1902 Palliser wrote to the Chairman of the Pacific Exploration Company, offering to reveal where the treasure was, in return for a quarter of the amount to be recovered for himself and one twentieth for his agent.[10] He relied on his reputation and his experience to win him a place on this new expedition; but

---

7 *Dundee Evening Telegraph*, 2 August 1904.

8 Hancock & Weston, 45 (maps), 308-9 (Fitzgerald).

9 Hancock & Weston, 122. See also *Sunderland Daily Echo and Shipping Gazette*, 8 September 1903; and *Derry Journal*, 11 September 1903.

10 *Dundee Evening Post*, 5 April 1902.

he also seems to have been guilty of some exaggeration, if the reporter from the *Dundee Evening Post* can be believed: 'Admiral Palliser [had] found the treasure and, not being able to carry a great quantity away he blasted a great deal of neighbouring rock with dynamite, and thus hid the spot where he had been working. ' The reporter then brought his readers down to earth

'The story of a member of the Metropolitan Fire Brigade, who was a seaman on HMS *Impérieuse*, and one of Admiral Palliser's working party at Cocos Island, was a little different. He told a reporter that Admiral Palliser never found the treasure. He found a stone slab, and then the water rushed in and washed the diggers out. Admiral Palliser blew up the ground with dynamite, not because he had found so much treasure that he couldn't carry it away, but in pure vexation because he couldn't find the treasure.'

Palliser's second expedition seems to have had no more success than the first; but he made a third, on board the *Lytton*, in 1903. The origin of this adventure lay in a plan made by a fellow Royal Naval officer with the intimidating name of Captain Shrapnel. Shrapnel and a friend called Grant planned to hire a steamship in Panama and sail from there to the Cocos, a distance of only 520 miles.[11] In the autumn of 1902, they formed a syndicate and were joined by Hervey de Montmorency, who recorded their adventures in a lively account entitled *On the Track of A Treasure*, published in London in 1904. Montmorency describes the qualities required of anyone who wanted to take part

'The treasure-seeker should be one who reserves in some dark cell of his recollections the memory of his school-boy days, when he read his Captain Marryat with relish, and followed with sparkling enthusiasm the fates of Mayne Reid's heroes. [He] should be a man who can be a boy again when he reads Robert Louis Stevenson.'

---

11 In a report in the *Tamworth Herald* for 14 January 1905, Shrapnel rather than Palliser is named as the commander of the Royal Navy's raid on Cocos Island in 1897. 'Shrapnel shell' is named after an artillery officer, Major-General Henry Shrapnel (1761–1842): wikipedia.

The syndicate did a deal with some Liverpool ship owners who wanted to carry cement to the Pacific coast of Mexico. The Liverpudlians bought a steamship from the Anchor Line and this was renamed the *Lytton*. On 1 May 1903 the Costa Rican ambassador in Paris gave permission to search for treasure on Cocos Island for 12 months, to the exclusion of all rival expeditions, provided that his government should receive one half of the profits; and the *Lytton* sailed for Swansea to pick up coal and Antwerp to collect cement.

The explorers, however, were not on board because they had arranged to meet up with their ship in Salina Cruz in Mexico. Instead Montmorency, Shrapnel and two others boarded *La Normandie*, of the *Compagnie Transatlantique*, at St Nazaire in France. They greatly enjoyed the superior service, food and wine to be found on French steamers. They called at Santander and La Coruña in Spain. They reached Florida on 4 July and they arrived in Vera Cruz on the Gulf of Mexico on 7 July, when they reported that 67 cases of yellow fever ('Yellow Jack') had recently been admitted to the local hospital.

They travelled overland via Mexico City, to Salina Cruz on the Pacific, After several hair-raising adventures with giant frogs, an especially hazardous railway line and bandits, they reached their destination. There, the engine-driver wished them goodbye, saying 'I hope you may find treasure.' When asked how he knew about the treasure, he remarked

> "Oh! We all know the *Lytton* is bound for Cocos Island, and no one goes there for any other purpose."

The explorers were supposed to rendezvous with their ship on 21 July 1903, but she was late and the terms of her hire had to be re-negotiated. They left the mainland on 4 August but did not enjoy the last leg of their journey, since their new berth was rust-eaten, cramped and 'carried a heavy passenger list of flies.' Indeed, she compared very unfavourably with *La Normandie* in every respect, including her rate of progress. The *Lytton* took almost five days to reach Cocos Island.

Montmorency and Co. made landfall in Chatham Bay on Cocos on 9 August, and were immediately struck by the natural beauty of the Island; but they could also see clearly that there were large numbers of sharks and enormous 'skates' (or rays) in the deep water. They spent nine days in an exhausting search for the treasure, but the Island was mountainous and overgrown, the climate was extremely wet and the streams which poured out of the jungle had eroded the natural features described in their Clues. They found nothing. They decided to return to Panama, but sailed round the headland to Wafer Bay before doing so.

Here they found some corrugated iron huts, and the Costa Rican colours flying from a flagpole. This was the home of August Gissler, the German who had first started looking for treasure in 1889, and had been appointed Governor by the Costa Ricans in 1897, but had been away when Palliser landed that year. Gissler had tried to establish a German colony but by 1903 all his colonists had left, leaving Gissler alone with his indomitable wife and a servant.[12] Nevertheless he had constructed a comfortable house and seemed largely self-sufficient. He grew bananas, oranges, limes, vines, pines, potatoes, yams, maize and other fruits and vegetables, as well as coffee; and he made cigars from his own tobacco, rope from banana fibre, while the tannic acid he made from the bark of a tulip tree was used to make ink and tan the hides of wild pigs.[13]

Montmorency thought Gissler 'a man of resource and invention', a modern Robinson Crusoe, who had suffered much at the hands of other explorers. His cows had been killed by the *Blakeley* expedition of 1902. The Royal Navy and others had ruined the landscape and allegedly vandalised his little farm. Accordingly he had good reason to be wary of strangers. Nevertheless he welcomed Montmorency and his party and was remarkably open about the great project of his life. Gissler had collected every clue and sifted every piece of evidence. Over the years, he had dug a complex system of tunnels (some of which still exist). He remained convinced that, with extra investment, he could find what he had been looking for. Yet, in all the years he had been looking, he had only found six gold coins; and he had now given up the last vestiges of hope and was resolved to leave the Island, which he did, on 23 August, 1903.

Montmorency saw no sign of any rival party while he was on Cocos Island. Furthermore, he expressed no wish in his book to return there. Indeed he saw

---

12 Hancock & Weston, 113, 305.

13 *Dundee Evening Post*, 12 January 1905.

little point. If Gissler couldn't find the treasure, no one else could. The reader is left to wonder whether Gissler or Montmorency (or both of them?) was holding something back because, in truth, neither was ready to give up their quest as yet. The part played by Henry Palliser in Montmorency's expedition of 1903 is obscure. What we do know is that in the following year Palliser was made Admiral, and met Earl Fitzwilliam. Together, they conceived a plan for yet another voyage, to be undertaken after the end of the rainy season on Cocos Island in November 1904.[14] The Earl would provide some miners and a ship, and obtain permission from the Costa Rican government. The Admiral would provide the crew, the seamanship and the all-important map.

---

14 Montmorency, 44.

Chapter 2

THE EARL AND THE ADMIRAL

William Charles de Meuron Wentworth-Fitzwilliam, the 7th Earl Fitzwilliam (1872 – 1943) succeeded to the earldom on the death of his grandfather, the 6th Earl, in 1902; and he was one of the richest men in Britain. He had several estates in England and in what we now call the Republic of Ireland. He owned the coal which lay in abundance under his principal seat in Wentworth in the West Riding of Yorkshire, as well as the mining equipment, some of the railways, and the houses and cottages inhabited by hundreds of miners and agricultural workers. Fitzwilliam maintained a stud to provide race-horses and hunters. He had a priceless art-collection and a 50-room house in Mayfair.[15] This is a man who would probably be worth around £3,000,000,000 in today's money; but he controlled the lives of those who worked for him to an extent which would be unthinkable in 2016, even for a billionaire.

The Earl's principal mansion was Wentworth Woodhouse, a truly enormous edifice built by his ancestors in the 18th century. Still standing today, it has a frontage some 600 feet wide, and is by some measures the largest house in England.[16] The guide will tell you that it has around 1,000 windows and an uncountable number of rooms, perhaps 365, depending on what one regards as a

---

15 Bailey, 7; *Nottingham Evening Post*, 12 February 1907; Sheffield Archives, Wentworth Woodhouse Muniments, T93, cited by *British History Online*.

16 Bailey, xxi.

room. There are several stories about Wentworth Woodhouse which emphasize, even exaggerate, its size. In 1910 an American visitor is said to have remarked

'It is a place so huge that guests find it of advantage to bring with them treble the ordinary number of hats, which are kept at the various entrances, so as to save themselves the trouble of walking about a quarter of a mile from one entrance in order to get the hat which they may have left at another.'[17]

Another story, related by a national newspaper in 1931, concerned the basement and vaults. Supposedly one of the Countesses Fitzwilliam had advised her husband that it was his duty to know every part of his house in great detail. He had confessed that he knew very little about the geography of the nether regions, and undertook a voyage of exploration, by way of penance.

'For what seemed to him like a very long time he groped his way along passages and through cellars without encountering any human being. At last he came across a smallish boy and asked him what might be his function in the establishment. "Me?" said the boy, "Why, I do all the work as is done in this place, don't I?" Upon that, Lord Fitzwilliam decided that he had, as it were, discovered the mainspring of his household, and retired to the upper regions.'[18]

In 1937 the 'Court and Society' column of another national newspaper informed its readers that

'Nervous guests are reputed to have tried the experiment of having a paper trail along passages to guide them back to their rooms; and another tale is that, during Doncaster week, when the host and hostess always entertain a large party, a manservant decided to test the distance covered while performing his duties, and his four days' work registered over fifty miles on a pedometer.'[19]

---

17 *Northampton Mercury*, 16 September 1910.

18 *The Manchester Guardian*, 10 December 1931.

19 *The Observer*, 12 September 1937.

The stable block at Wentworth Woodhouse, built by John Carr of York between 1768 and 1779 to accommodate 84 horses, is itself so large that it is sometimes mistaken for the mansion, while the wall surrounding Wentworth Park is nine miles long. In and around it are several large follies, including Hoober Stand, Keppel's Column, the Needle's Eye and the Mausoleum, perfect examples of what a later age would call 'conspicuous consumption'. In the 6th Earl's time, there were 84 servants at 'the Big House.' A photograph, taken in 1890, shows a housekeeper and 8 maids. Another, taken ten years later, shows 60 out-door and non-domestic staff. A third, taken in 1902, shows 11 woodyard staff; but there were also gardeners, park-keepers, deer keepers, gamekeepers, grooms, poultry men and many others. Wentworth Woodhouse saw no less than three royal visits, in 1886, 1891 and 1912.

The 7th Earl was regarded, in British public school terms, as both a 'good egg' and an 'all-rounder'. He was educated at Eton and Cambridge, where he was Master of the Trinity College Beagles and won a Blue in point-to-point racing. He was an Army Officer in India (1893–94) and in South Africa during the Boer War (1899-1902). He sat in the House of Lords and was an experienced mining engineer, a sportsman interested in racing and golf, and a pioneer motorist who held a car rally in Wentworth Park as early as 1903.

Despite their enormous wealth and power, successive owners of Wentworth Woodhouse enjoyed a reputation as being on the reformist wing of British politics. They were Whigs and then Liberals. The 2nd Marquis of Rockingham opposed George III and supported the demands of the colonists during the American War of Independence (1776-1783), and was Prime Minister twice. His nephew, the 4th Earl Fitzwilliam, inherited his uncle's estates and assumed his position in the Whig party, resigning as Lord Lieutenant of Ireland in 1795, when George III refused to countenance any measure of relief for Roman Catholics, from their civil disabilities. The Whig and Liberal tradition survived until the late 19th century, when it foundered on the rock of Gladstone's advocacy of Home Rule for Ireland. The 7th Earl became a Conservative and was M.P. for Wakefield between 1895 and 1902, when he took his seat in the House of Lords.

The Fitzwilliam family also had a solid reputation for hospitality and philanthropy. Shortly after the marriage of the future 8th Earl in 1933, *The Manchester Guardian* published a story which traced the origin of this reputation back to the Tudor period

'Lord Milton, who is heir to the longest private house in England, is [also heir to] one of the most famous of all the great Whig family traditions – he has Cavendish and Ponsonby and Wentworth blood – and to a splendid reputation for hospitality. It was one of the earliest of Fitzwilliams who set up in the High Street of Sprotborough a cross with the words engraven on brass

"Who is hungry and lists to eate,
Let him come to Sprotobrough to his meate;
And for a night, and for a day,
His horse shall have both corn and hay."

When Wolsey fell, he gave him hospitality in Milton. Called to account by the King, he replied that he had done what befitted his honour for his old master and part founder of his fortune. The King liked the answer well enough to make Fitzwilliam a Privy Councillor.'[20]

The Fitzwilliam family continued to enjoy its favourable reputation in the 19th and early 20th centuries, despite the radical changes in master-servant relationships brought about by the Industrial Revolution and the advent of democracy. Indeed, they were regarded with respect and affection even in the South of Ireland, where hatred of the Protestant Ascendancy ran deep. Many country houses belonging to the British aristocracy went up in flames during the Irish War of Independence of 1919-21; but Coolattin House and Carnew Castle still stand.

---

20 *The Manchester Guardian*, 20 April, 1933.

The 7th Earl inherited the Fitzwilliam title in 1902, when he was 30, and travelled to Cocos Island only two years later. Where did his interest in exploration spring from, and why was he prepared to spend months away from home in pursuit of it? After all, he lacked a male heir in 1904. He had three daughters, but they could not inherit his title or his landed estates. If he died without producing a son, the earldom and all his real property would pass to another branch – as was to happen in 1948 and again in 1952, or die out altogether, as ultimately happened in 1979.

There were a number of reasons for his passion for adventure. His father (who died in 1877 and never became Earl) had been a great traveller, and wrote an extensive account of his journey through the Rocky Mountains, published as *The North-West Passage by Land.*[21] Fitzwilliam had himself been born at *Pointe de Meuron* in the Canadian wilderness in 1872, where he had acquired his unusual Christian name. The circumstances of his birth had even led to a major controversy within the family. The accusation was made that he was a changeling, an unrelated baby secretly inserted into the line of succession. In 1902 some members of the family even went so far as to try to exclude him from his inheritance, though the case never went to court, because Fitzwilliam faced them all down.[22] He showed a determination then which was to serve him well in future years.

In the years before and after 1900, there was a vogue for adventure stories of all kinds and *Treasure Island*, by Robert Louis Stevenson, was now an international bestseller. Some people have even speculated that Stevenson's story was set on Cocos Island, despite the many differences in topography.[23] But Stevenson was not the only contemporary to show an interest in pirates and buried treasure at this time. There was also J.M.Barrie, whose stage play *Peter Pan* was premiered in London at Christmas 1904, the very time when Fitzwilliam's expedition was in the Pacific. Indeed, the early 20th century saw a renewed interest in exploration, particularly of the Antarctic. Sir Clements Markham was President of the Royal Geographical Society between 1893 and 1905 and

---

21 Young, 39; Bailey, 24.

22 Young, 39, Bailey, chapter 7.

23 Smith, 843; the *Sunday Post*, 14 May 1922.

he encouraged Scott and Shackleton to undertake their famous voyages to the far South although, as far as we know, he had no dealings with Earl Fitzwilliam.

The party of explorers which Fitzwilliam put together in 1904 consisted very largely of his servants and employees, apart from Palliser, who was very much his own man. There was Captain North, Master of the Horse at Wentworth Woodhouse; Frank Brooke, Fitzwilliam's Irish estate agent and a resident and magistrate in the village of Shillelagh; 'Mr' Bulkeley (whose occupation and role remain mysterious); and St John Durnford, who was a mining engineer. There was also one friend and one relative in the company; and, last but not least, there was a group of miners from the collieries around Wentworth. One pitman was called 'Fowler'; but we do not know the names of the others.

The friend was George Eustace Cooke-Yarborough, a younger son from one of the oldest families in Yorkshire, whose seat was at Campsmount in Campsall, north of Doncaster. Always known as Eustace, he was educated at Charterhouse and Magdalen College Oxford and was called to the Bar in 1900. He practised law on the Northern Circuit and had his Chambers in Leeds. He was 28 in 1904. The relative was David Smith, whose elder brother, Lt.-Colonel William Mackenzie Smith (b. 1869) had married Fitzwilliam's older sister, Lady Mabel (b. 1870). Lady Mabel would have been considered a 'character' in any age. She had turned to politics because her brother 'had so much' and everyone else 'had so little', and was thought to be 'a rabid socialist'. Perhaps she salved her conscience by marrying Mackenzie Smith, whose mansion at Barnes Hall, Bracken Hill only had 18 bedrooms.[24]

When the party assembled in Southampton, the Earl bought a ship named *Harlech Castle* and re-named her *Véronique,* after a popular French musical which was playing in the town. She was a steamship once used on the mail run to South America. With the crew recruited by the Admiral, the total number on board was around 60. Her destination was not disclosed to the public, nor was the true purpose of the journey. Indeed David Smith tells us that the whole crew, including the Earl's closest companions, were sworn to secrecy from the very beginning

---

24 Bailey, family tree, p x, 401-2. For Barnes Hall, see Eastwood's *Ecclesfield.*

'Nobody but our leader knew the exact location until we were well out at sea. Every precaution had been taken to keep our departure and purpose secret. Not one of us left an address behind to which letters could be forwarded.'[25]

The 'destination' and 'purpose' of the voyage of the *Véronique* was never fully disclosed by Fitzwilliam, even after he returned home; but it is now possible to give an authoritative account, thanks to the ability of the young barrister, Eustace Cooke-Yarborough, to record what he saw with his own eyes, and record it accurately.

---

25 Smith, 843.

Chapter 3

THE VOYAGE

Eustace kept a journal whilst on the voyage and must have maintained a lively interest in the adventure for some time afterwards, because it contains photographs, postcards, two menus prepared on board the ship he came home in, and telegrams and cuttings from British newspapers published in 1905 and 1906. He tells us at the outset that they were bound for Cocos Island, and their expedition had a wider purpose than his friend Fitzwilliam ever willingly admitted. This was

> 'to explore that island and certain portions of the adjacent mainland for coal and other minerals and at the same time to attempt the discovery of a treasure supposed to be hidden on the island.'

Eustace's list of those on board *Véronique* includes a Jersey cow, although David Smith described her as an Alderney. Whichever she was, she became a working member of the expedition, because 'Tinned milk did not appeal to some of the buccaneers.' She lived in a loose-box on deck.

They left Southampton on a calm day, 21 October 1904, but Eustace also tells us that they all knew, before they ever embarked, that the *Véronique* was a 'roller'; and all except the sailors dreaded the crossing of the notorious Bay of Biscay. However, they decided to enjoy their dinners on the first night out of

Plymouth, though the *Véronique* had already 'begun to show that she intended to act up to her reputation.'

On Sunday 23 October the ship started to roll 'horribly'. Next day, when they passed Cape Finisterre, she began rolling even more. When Eustace went down to dinner, 'an even bigger roll than usual sent the Doctor, who was in a loose chair, flying across the saloon.' This was too much for our narrator and he fled, leaving David Smith, the Admiral and the Captain alone at table.[26]

Almost everyone was ill next day; but then the *Véronique* began to pitch and roll by turns. Someone continued to take photographs; but Eustace noted a terrible contrast now between the cry of "All's well", as the hours were rung at night, and the plight they were truly in. Smith remarked that "N" (North?) suffered more than anyone. Indeed, he showed little signs of life, beyond issuing 'gurgling appeals for soda and brandy.' Even the Jersey cow grew sick and would eat nothing. She was treated by Bulkeley but it was Smith who solved the problem, thought to be constipation, using the unsavoury but effective method of 'back-raking'. The result was that the cow 'got her sea-legs, could take exercise in any but very unfavourable weather and milked well.'[27]

The men suffered terribly in the Bay of Biscay, but things began to improve as they passed Madeira and the sea became calmer. They felt much better as they admired the great cliffs; and by Sunday 30 October the officers and crew were putting on their white drill uniforms. They held a Church Parade at 10.30 a.m. and said Prayers in the Captain's Saloon. On 31 October they reached San Antonio, the first of the Cape Verde Islands. Everyone thought that the harbour was splendid, though Eustace exclaimed 'What a country to live in! Eustace was a typical Englishman of his day. He did not much like foreigners, and used the sort of language which would nowadays land anyone, from politician to footballer, in a good deal of trouble. After describing the awesome volcanic scenery on St. Vincent, he turned his attention to the human geography.

---

26 Yet Smith's obituary in1960 stated that he spent a year in Switzerland when he was young, for his health.

27 Smith, 844.

'The population consists of about 7,000 n------s, half a dozen Portuguese and 150 white men nearly all of the latter clerks in the Telegraph Department or agents for coaling firms. How white men exist in such a place one cannot imagine. We were there in the cool season, but the place was then a fiery furnace.'

It was on another of the Cape Verde Islands that they heard that war might be about to break out, between Great Britain and Imperial Russia. This was because the Russian Baltic Fleet had entered the North Sea as they left Southampton, on its way to tackle the Japanese; and, by mistake, it had fired on British trawlers. Three British fishermen had been killed and, for a time, it looked as if His Majesty's Government would take reprisals. Those on board *Véronique* seem to have been all in favour of this; and they were not alone. David Smith tells us that, while the *Véronique* was off the north coast of Spain, a Royal Navy cruiser asked her to alter course so that the tars could 'save the Japanese the trouble', by opening fire on the Russians. It was only when they crossed the Equator that our friends heard that there would be no war.[28]

Otherwise, that week was uneventful. They spent all day taking on coal at St Vincent, while some of them went fishing, using beef as bait, catching two red mullets and a conger eel. Just before they left the Cape Verde Islands, Bulkeley brought a one-eyed white terrier on board, which he had purchased from a 'negress'. Later on, they had some trouble when the terrier insisted on fighting the ship's cat.[29]

The ship began to average over 250 miles a day. The sea was calm and the weather hot. Shoals of flying fish darted away constantly from the side of the ship. On 3 November they all drank the health of the Japanese Emperor. Otherwise, they were beginning to find it difficult to occupy their time; and some were even bored. Then, on 13 November, they noticed that the colour of the sea had changed from blue to green, and realised that this must be due

---

28 When the Russian fleet eventually reached the Far East, it was sent to the bottom by the Imperial Japanese Navy.

29 Smith, 844.

to their nearing the River Plate, though the ship was still some 450 miles from their next port of call.

Smith tells us that they were refused entry to Rio de Janeiro because of civil unrest there, the result of a dispute between two political parties concerning vaccination. On 16 November, they dropped anchor in Montevideo in Uruguay. Eustace did not think much of the place.

> 'Uninteresting town. Streets all at right angles. The country in chronic state of revolution, which paralyzes trade. Two parties, red and white, always at one another's throats. On the smallest pretext, the party in opposition rises, and devotes itself to the wholesale destruction of the property of members of the government faction, which is promptly followed by counter-destruction by the party in power.'

On the other hand, the reporter from the *Montevideo Times* had a high opinion of Fitzwilliam's party, though he laboured under certain misapprehensions as to who they all were. The Earl had spread the word that he was the leader of a scientific expedition in search of orchids; and the local reporter bought this idea, writing that a 'distinguished party' had arrived, which included Captain Bulkeley, Captain Smith, Professor Durnford, Professor Yarborough, and Dr Ainger. [30]

Whilst in Montevideo, Eustace and Durnford went off on a paddle-steamer to Buenos Aires in Argentina, where there was 'sound government', and where they were shown around, went to the races, visited the Flower Corso, and bought postcards. They were interviewed there by another journalist, who made the same mistake as his Uruguayan colleague, in thinking that the treasure-hunters were academics engaged in a programme of serious study.

Eustace thought that Buenos Aires was 'a splendid town'; but he found it expensive, and was disappointed that there were so many strikes. He thought that most of the trade was 'falling into the hands of German firms, who seem to be ousting the English in everything except the cattle trade.' He and Durnford

---

30 Smith, 845.

returned to the ship in the early hours of Saturday 19 November; and the *Véronique* left Montevideo at midnight next day.

The ship resumed its course for the South. At one point, Eustace saw once again a distinct line in the Ocean, with water of a different colour on either side of it, but this time the phenomenon was caused by a current rather than the proximity of a great river. He was clearly captivated by the grandeur and strangeness of his surroundings.

At some point they picked up a pilot and on 25 November they entered the Straits of Magellan, before circumnavigating the tip of South America, so they did not 'round the Horn', as some would later claim. Nor were they entering uncharted waters. Until the Panama Canal opened in 1914, the Straits of Magellan were the main route for steamships travelling from the Atlantic to the Pacific; and the port of Punta Arenas in Chile, the southernmost city in the world, was a major coaling station.

They took four days to negotiate the Straits; and in an inlet called Porto Bueno they decided to go hunting, for deer, duck and geese for their larder; but the trip proved a disaster. They returned to the ship wet through and covered in slime, having bagged only a hawk and a cormorant. However, Eustace tells us that they enjoyed the exercise, and the scenery was very beautiful, somewhat resembling the Kyles of Bute. David Smith was also reminded of Scotland although, in his account of the hunting trip, they had to wade through 'terrain resembling elephantine custard pudding, covered with giant macaroni and asparagus.'

According to Smith again, the most remarkable sight they saw when passing through the Straits of Magellan, was a Scotsman who was working as a trapper on Tierra del Fuego. This gentleman was said to have five wives, and hoisted the Union Jack as they passed.

They entered the Pacific, where they saw several albatross. The great Ocean was calm and they picked up speed as they now headed North. They began to average 250 miles a day once more; but, on the night of 2 December, the ship started to roll again, at one time by as much as 44 degrees. On this occasion, no-one was seasick but the pilot 'was much astonished at [the ship's] capacity for rolling. He said she beat the small coal tramps hollow.' Eustace added that 'the captain, while sitting in a big armchair in his cabin, was chucked right over onto the floor.' They still notched up another 269 miles that day.

The next stop was Valparaiso in Chile, where they again encouraged the locals to believe that they were distinguished scientists. For a change, Eustace liked the place.

'The old town in its irregularity forms a great contrast to the new towns of Monte Video and Buenos Aires on the other side of the continent, with their streets all straight and at regular intervals cutting one another at right angles.'

He also commented that the English were losing out, once again, commercially. 'A good many English and Germans live here and in business matters the Germans especially are to the fore.'

They were given a box at the opera and shown all the sights, but they did not stay long; and they then spent ten uneventful days heading due North for Panama. On 12 December, with the aid of a strong current, they notched up a total of 300 miles.

Eustace informs us that 'the Republic of Panama has been practically swallowed up by America', since it was the Americans who had just begun cutting the Panama Canal. He also relates the curious fact that the Pacific Ocean was at a 'considerably higher level than the Atlantic' and people feared that, if the Canal were cut without locks, 'the two Oceans would level one another in a day'(!) Smith tells us that, when they went ashore in Panama, they took the precaution of wrapping their ankles in bandages and taking large doses of quinine, for fear of the Yellow Jack. Six Americans who ignored the advice to do so were dead within 48 hours.[31]

Whilst in Panama they went hunting for shark, and not just any shark, but a particular fish which had recently killed a little girl. As usual, they lacked the necessary equipment. After a long struggle, in which the shark nearly dragged two members of the fishing party into the sea, they managed to get a line around

---

31 Smith, 845-6.

'the brute' and winch him aboard; but they had to beat a retreat when he started lashing about the deck, snapping his jaws like 'an angry wolf'. When they cut him open, they found a brass knob inside him, as big as a bedstead's.

On 17 December they left Panama and two days later, after a further 470 miles, they reached Puntarenas in Costa Rica. Imagine their feelings when they found that the British yacht *Rose Marine* was already anchored there! Eustace tells us that they knew full well that a rival expedition had set out for the Island before them, but they had not expected to find them here in Costa Rica. It soon became apparent that Hervey de Montmorency had returned, this time in the company of one Harold S. Gray, 'a well-known and wealthy sportsman', and said to be a friend of Palliser's.[32] Montmorency proceeded to inform them that his party had already landed on Cocos Island, and still had a dozen Spanish navvies (or 'peons') at work there. Moreover, he said that he had obtained a concession from the Costa Ricans, giving him exclusive rights to search for the treasure.

One might have expected a fight to break out then and there, or at least that a certain frostiness might develop; but both sides seem to have possessed typically stiff upper lips. The two parties of British explorers remained on speaking terms, though they were mutually suspicious; but serious doubt had now been cast on the nature and validity of the permission which Fitzwilliam had obtained. Accordingly, at 4 o'clock on 17 December, the Earl, Brooke, Dr Brady, Carter and North left the port to travel up to San José, in order to see the President of Costa Rica. Eustace did not accompany them,[33] nor did Smith, so we do not have a first-hand account of this journey into the hinterland; but we do know that the first and third legs had to be made by train, and the second required mules, since San José lies at 4,000 feet and the going was very difficult.

While Fitzwilliam was away, some of those left behind decided to go shooting on the islands in the gulf. To this end they took a launch, linked up with an American known as 'Mr Max', and visited the Governor of a penal colony on St Luke's Island. This gentleman invited them for breakfast; but the British did not

---

32 *Tamworth Herald*, 14 January 1905.

33 Eustace's grandson Anthony Cooke-Yarborough remembers his saying or recording 'Today Fitzwilliam went ashore to interview the President', which perhaps reflected his grandfather's perception of the two men's relative importance.

know what they had let themselves in for. Eustace records that 'the Governor allowed us to refuse nothing'. The breakfast consisted of

1. Macaroni soup
2. Fried eggs and boiled rice
3. Pork chops
4. Leg of pork with whole baked plantains
5. Pork cutlets with onions and strips of baked plantains
6. Black beans
7. Sweets. Some fruit cut in strips, very sweet.
8. Coffee & cigarettes.'

Eustace adds

'It was exceedingly kind and hospitable of the Governor, but we should have been quite satisfied with ¼ of the feast. I think he was very glad to have some company to entertain for he has a dull time on the island.'

He goes on to record the extraordinary liberty the prisoners enjoyed on this island, whilst pointing out that it was surrounded by sharks, so there was no possibility of escape. The hunting party then steamed round to the other side of the island, where they spied an alligator asleep on a mud bank. This created considerable confusion in the ranks, even panic; and, when the creature seemed to be waking up, they fired several shots at it, missing completely. After shooting a few small birds, they made their way back to the ship for dinner. Eustace had enjoyed the day so much that he felt moved to pen some doggerel.

'Though there was nought to bring away at last
When the hunters' day was done.
We'd paraded up and down a bit
And had a rattlin' day'

Next day, 21 December, some of our brave hunters went off again in the launch and steamed up the creek where they had seen the alligator. They chased some birds which resembled English plovers, except that they had webbed feet. They got stuck on a mud bank several times, but managed to bag 2½ brace of web-footed plover, 7 brace of parrots and a single iguana. They ate the parrots for breakfast; and Eustace informs us that they made 'excellent eating'.

On 22 December they received a telegram from Fitzwilliam to say that he would not be returning from San José until the 23rd. They decided to have another day's hunting, and this time to camp out overnight. We saw that the men on board the *Véronique* remained on speaking terms with the men from the *Rose Marine*; but it still comes as a surprise to learn that, when Eustace and his fellows set off on this further shooting expedition, some of their rivals, including Montmorency himself, were invited to come along. The happy band of brothers called on the Governor of the prison at St Luke's island again; and asked for permission to make camp and shoot deer. The Governor tried to insist that they all stay with him for the night but, as Eustace records

'Wishing to be independent and fearing that most of our time might be spent in devouring enormous meals similar to the one had had already given us, we declined, with many thanks for his hospitality.'

The combined group of hunters got their pilot to drop them on the mainland, about two miles from the place where they intended to camp. They waded ashore and made their way inland, past a deserted Indian house. They frightened some parrots, which flew off; but not before Eustace had let off an 'ineffectual' shot. They walked on for a quarter of an hour when the pilot, who was now acting as guide, stopped in his tracks, pointed into the bush, seized hold of a gun from the nearest man, and fired. He missed, but they heard some unknown animal dash away into the undergrowth. The guide pursued it, found that it had gone into a hole, found a second hole which he assumed to be the creature's escape route and immediately began to stuff the exit with leaves, to which he set fire, with the intention of smoking the beast out. After twenty minutes, out came an armadillo, which Carter shot and killed. It was, in Eustace's words, 'a fine armadillo'; but Carter's marksmanship had nearly severed its head from its body. He does not say whether they ate it. They found no other game that day; and returned to their campsite. They had tea outdoors and it grew dark at 6 o'clock; but it was difficult to rest. 'The beetles commenced their din, a weird sort of a noise something between a hiss and a whirr!'

Since there was nothing to do, and they intended to rise at 5.30 next morning, the party turned in at 8.30, but found that their tent had been invaded by hermit crabs. So much for Bulkeley's expertise in erecting it! They ejected the intruders and piled sand round the edge of the tent to keep them from re-entering, but the noise of crabs trying to break into the tent, along with the sound of the beetles, kept them awake all night. Their only consolation was that they were not also attacked by mosquitoes or red ants, as they had expected to be. Then, at 2 a.m. someone realised that the tide was coming in and, by 3 a.m., water was lapping all around the tent. At 4.30, they got up, had tea and biscuits and waited for the sun to rise.

They must have been exhausted by now, but they still set off in pursuit of deer next day; and Eustace paired off with Durnford. They marched for two hours but found nothing, except for some small birds which they decided to leave alone. They returned to camp for breakfast and the whole party returned to the mainland, where they found the Indian house they had come across the day before. They bought a dog there, thinking it might be useful for hunting pigs. Presumably they thought the one-eyed terrier unfitted for the task.

Fitzwilliam arrived back on Christmas Eve. It seemed that he had solved the problem of competing concessions; and the whole party celebrated Christmas Day 1904 on board *Véronique*. There was no hostility towards those on board the *Rose Marine* and Fitzwilliam even invited Montmorency over to Christmas Dinner; but Eustace tells it was a very sober affair. Perhaps the climate prevented them from enjoying the festivities, since it was 90 degrees in the shade. In any event, *Véronique* departed for Cocos Island on Boxing Day.

Chapter 4

THE EXPLOSION

Montmorency's account shows that, in some respects, he had been much better prepared in 1903, than Fitzwilliam was in 1904. In fact, it makes Fitzwilliam look like the amateur he was; but there is no indication that the two British teams pooled their knowledge when they encountered one another on the Costa Rican mainland at Christmas 1904. On the contrary, neither side was willing to help the other, though (as Eustace Cooke-Yarborough realised) this was an age when the British were suffering intense competition from Germany and the United States in almost every field of endeavour. One consequence of this was that Fitzwilliam was unaware that the Costa Ricans had granted concessions to Gissler and Montmorency which conflicted with his own.

Fitzwiliam had none of the three Clues used by Montmorency in 1903 but he had Palliser's map. Accordingly, the *Véronique* dropped anchor in Chatham Bay on Cocos Island on 27 December 1904, intending to land 30 men near the supposed site of the treasure, while the ship sailed back to Panama to fetch the mail and other things. Eustace tells us that the Earl, the Admiral and Frank Brooke went ahead to see if they could recognise any feature described in Palliser's map; but, after spending half an hour slipping and sliding around, they were forced to return to the ship's boat, in search of a better landing-place, and somewhere to pitch the tents.

This did not prove to be easy. With the aid of field-glasses, they could all see that the land rose steeply from the sea on all sides and was almost entirely covered with dense vegetation. Moreover, although there were numerous streams, these became waterfalls at the shoreline. Reconnaissance was going to be difficult; and they could see only one small piece of level sand which would be suitable for a campsite. They had four boats: a steam launch, a motor boat, a gig or rowing boat and a small shore boat which they had purchased in Costa Rica. The heavy surf meant that they could only get near the beach in the shore boat, and even then, only to a point where the rollers began to break. Then they had to jump into the water, up to their waists. This they did, but somewhat nervously, because they had seen large numbers of sharks in the water and, as Eustace noted

> 'Beyond the fact that there were a good number of us splashing about,
> there was nothing to prevent one of the brutes coming into the 3 or 4
> ft. of water that we were compelled to stand in.'

He seems to have blissfully unaware that splashing about in the water was more likely to attract sharks than repel them.

By now it was 3.30p.m. The motor boat broke down and could not be used to ferry goods from the *Véronique* to the shore boat. This meant that several operations were involved in depositing the gear on the sand. They had to transfer it from the ship to a lifeboat; tow the lifeboat with the steam-launch; transfer it from the lifeboat to the gig; row the gig in a bit further; transfer it from the gig to the shore-boat; get the shore-boat in as far as safely possible; and finally man-haul it through the surf. There must have been a better way; but they did not find it. As Eustace wrote, 'under these conditions, it took an hour or two to unload even one lifeboat full'. We can hear the weariness in his voice; but he added that there was yet a further stage to their Calvary.

'When the stuff had been deposited on shore, it then had to be carried a quarter of a mile to where the camp was to be, and the way lay over huge boulders on which it was hard to keep one's footing. In addition to this the tide was coming in and making the narrow strip of beach still narrower every minute. And above the high water mark began the dense vegetation, with overhanging trees here and there, blocking our way over the boulders.'

They toiled all afternoon; but it grew dark before they had finished the business of unloading. Fitzwilliam was determined to press on, but Dr Brady called a halt to the torture, pointing out the risks involved in camping out before they had been able to unload all their equipment. Everyone but the Earl was keen to follow this advice, because it had been raining almost continuously and they could see no possibility of obtaining any comfort under canvas. Accordingly, they returned to the ship, changed into dry clothes and had a good dinner. The backbreaking work of unloading the *Véronique* began again next morning, 28 December. The tide had gone out, the weather was fine for a change, and they had a much larger stretch of beach to work on. Even so, it was midday before the job was done. Unloading the Jersey Cow was an especially delicate procedure. However

'the cow took the indignities of being prostrated in a small boat with her legs tied; and then being rolled out into the sea, in a most prosaic manner. She walked soberly ashore and immediately began to devour the fresh grass of which there was plenty. She made herself at home in no time and improved in condition wonderfully during the three days we were ashore.'

He might almost have said that she had a stiff upper lip!

The human members of the expedition enjoyed no such relief. Fitzwilliam and Durnford went off in a boat and entered a cave below the cliff, where the Admiral's map suggested that the treasure might be hidden; but they could not even gain an entrance, because the sea was too high and rough. The rest of the men allocated to shore duties made camp and had dinner at about 7.30p.m. Watches were set; but Eustace thought it a miserable job to be roused at 2 a.m. for his two hour stint. 'A damper place than where we were encamped it would have been impossible to find.' They were only a couple of feet above high water mark, there was a stream of water on either side of the tents, and the sand on which they were pitched was always wet. At this point in Eustace's narrative, there is a surprising development:

'Geissler [sic],[34] the Governor of the Island, told us that at spring tides the sea swept clear over the position we occupied.'

What is this? According to Montmorency's account, August Gissler had abandoned his colony in Wafer Bay and returned to Panama in 1903. Yet here he is, back on Cocos, in 1904;[35] and it is only now that Eustace tells us who he was and what he looked like, in much the same terms as Montmorency had done in his book. Both narrators thought he was a remarkable character, 'a tall finely made man, with a long brown beard and good features', who seemed to them like a living Robinson Crusoe.

Some three years later, in 1907, Gissler gave an interview to the *New York Times*, in which he gave his own account of his life on Cocos Island. It appears from this that he had eventually been given extremely wide powers by the Costa Rican government. When the reporter put it to him that he was in effect 'Governor, Colonel, the whole army, lord high executioner, judge, jury and undertaker', he did not deny it;[36] but he behaved impeccably towards the British in 1904, when he came across their makeshift camp. He asked the Earl who he was, where he had come from and what he wanted, although he also told him that, if he had come in search of treasure, he could not help him, as Montmorency's party already had a valid and exclusive concession. However,

---

34 The *Tamworth Herald*, 14 January 1905, has the spelling 'Geisleir'. The same newspaper has de Montmorency's first name as Herbert rather than Hervey.

35 According to the *Dundee Evening Post* for 12 January 1905, the German's reason for returning to the mainland in 1903 was simply that his wife had fallen and dislocated her shoulder. He did not abandon the island altogether until 1908.

36 Hancok & Weston, 306.

when Fitzwilliam replied that he had been given permission to land by the Costa Rican President, the German became amicable, and he and Fitzwilliam had a long conversation in private. We would love to have been flies on the wall.

Next day, 29 December, the shore party began to explore Chatham Bay, to see what they could find. Eustace was paired with the Doctor and, armed with a machete and a long curved knife, they set out to skirt the hillside around Chatham Bay. They soon came across a creek which they thought they could walk up; but this proved much more difficult than anticipated, since they had to hack every yard of the way through dense vegetation.

'It was most despairing work for we seemed to get "no forrader"[37] and were continually falling into holes, or slipping down steep banks. We were also much troubled by either some insect or stinging plant, which attacked us on our necks and caused a very painful smarting.'

They eventually beat a retreat down a ravine, and re-joined their friends empty handed, except for a hammer which Eustace found in the sand.

The next day was equally exhausting and frustrating for all concerned. They tried to land near the sea-cave which Durnford and Fitzwilliam had already entered, and failed again, the surf being even higher and rougher; but some of them spent some time clearing creepers and moss off a cliff, about a quarter of a mile from the camp, with a view to examining it for minerals. Smith's account tells us that the object of clearing the cliff was to expose the entrance to a cave system, where they hoped to find the long-lost hoard. In the afternoon, Gissler came over to their camp again and had another long interview with Fitzwilliam. We feel it unlikely that he was very encouraging.

New Year's Eve, 1904, was the fourth day after their arrival on the Island, and it proved to be their last. Eustace records that Bulkeley set out early, taking the Yorkshire miners along, as well as a 'N-----r or two'.[38] He wanted to start serious work at the cliff face, and more specifically to blast away the obstruc-

---

37 No further forward.
38 The *Northampton Mercury*, 13 January 1905 reported that Fitzwilliam had stopped to pick up labourers in Jamaica.

tions caused by a landslide. The problem he faced was well explained by the spokesman for another expedition to Cocos, upon his return to Britain: 'the torrential rains cause constant landslides, and when digging takes place, one landslide after another may ensue.'[39]

The miners set off two or three charges and returned for breakfast, then went back to the rock face. What happened next is best told by Eustace Cooke-Yarborough.

'It must have been about 10 o'clock or little before while the Doctor and I were sitting in the tent, speculating as to what time the *Véronique* would return – for it was on this morning that she was expected – that the cook came running up to the Doctor and said "I think they want you over there where they are blasting, I think there has been an accident."

'From where we were sitting we could not see the spot; but on running out we saw all the others hurrying together, and Fitzwilliam who was on the steam launch at the time was returning to the shore in the small boat. When we got to the place we saw that a lot of rocks had fallen down the hill and on climbing up we saw Bulkeley just being lifted up with his head all bleeding.'

All was silent, but only for a moment. Just as they might have thought that all was over, there was another tremendous explosion.

'I had got hold of his legs and several of us were just carrying him down the hill when there came a rumble and a roar and I felt myself being hurled down the slope. I felt a blow in the back which knocked me over and could hear rocks and stones rushing past me. I was wondering whereabouts I was going to be crushed when I suddenly realised that it was all over. On picking myself up I found myself some ten yards below where Bulkeley was lying. Beyond some bruises and cuts I was none the worse.'

---

39 *Tamworth Herald*, 14 January 1905.

The same could not be said for the others. Bulkeley had now been blown up twice. He was unconscious, had sustained a serious head injury, from which he was bleeding profusely, and his legs were trapped in the debris. Fitzwilliam, who had been blown up only once, was on his feet but his head was also streaming with blood. Colonel Carter had one leg jammed under a rock. Brooke was unable to move and was in great pain. The 'poor n-----r' was almost entirely buried, and appeared 'quite dead.' Lower down the slope, the steward Hester was in great distress, while higher up, near to the cliff which they had been blasting, there were two miners, trying to extract their mate from the rubble. This must have been Fowler. Eustace and the others who were uninjured set to work immediately, in order to help their comrades down the slope and out of danger, since they feared that there might be another landslip, if not a third explosion. It took a couple of hours before they all reached the tents. Eventually, the wounded were laid out on tables and the doctor began the grim work.

Eustace noted that Bulkeley was in most need of attention: his head wounds were severe and he nearly died; but Bowles had broken ribs and a broken collar bone, and was in so much pain that he begged them not to move him. On the other hand, the steward behaved as one would expect an English gentleman to behave. He had a broken leg and broken arms, but begged his rescuers to attend to others first. Colonel Carter had a sprained ankle, the 'n-----r' had several head injuries and a crushed hand, and the miner, Fowler, had dislocated his leg and sustained a wound so deep in his back 'that a man could put his hand in it'.

The wounded were transferred to the *Véronique,* where they were a good deal more comfortable, though they all spent a miserable New Year's Day, 1905. Nonetheless, most made a swift recovery. Within two days, Bowles was smoking a pipe, while Fowler was talking about his injuries as "Nobbut a poonch or two in t'back." According to later reports, Colonel Carter was left on board the ship for a time, but the others with serious injuries (Bowles, Hester and Fowler) were transferred to a hospital in Panama, where they were well looked after by American doctors.[40]

The question now was whether Fitzwilliam would attempt to resume the search on Cocos Island with his remaining able-bodied companions. Eustace tells us that most of these wanted to do so. In his eyes

> 'It seemed a great pity not to return to Cocos to try and do something, seeing that we had the ship and all the implements and gear there within two day's journey.'

This indicated that the true spirit of adventure had survived their ordeals; but Fitzwilliam was against the idea of having another 'go'. As Eustace explained, the Earl was 'so shocked at the whole affair that he decided to abandon any further attempts for now.' It is as well to bear this reaction in mind, when we consider his later attempts to cover up what had happened.

Fitzwilliam burnt his boats behind him now, by selling the *Véronique* to a German magnate and arranging for the able-bodied gentlemen in his party to return to England on board a Royal Mail Steamship called *Orinoco*.[41]

There is some confirmation of the Earl's continuing concern for his men in the four telegrams preserved with Eustace Cooke-Yarborough's Journal. Two of these were sent by Fitzwilliam himself to Eustace's father at Campsmount, and at the court house in Doncaster, where he sat as presiding magistrate, on 7 January 1905. They contained a comforting message

> 'Slight accident. All well. *Véronique* party returning. Arrive Southampton 26th.'

The other telegrams were sent two days later by the Earl's secretary Cecil Cowper in London, to Eustace's father and to the Warde-Aldams of Frickley

---

40 *Manchester Courier*, 10 January 1905; *Tamworth Herald*, 14 January 1905.

41 *Véronique* was captured by the Peruvians in 1915, renamed and finally broken up in 1943.

Hall near Doncatser, who were family friends, re-assuring them that Eustace was safe and well.[42]

For those on board *Orinoco*, the journey home from Colon in Panama to Britain was luxurious, especially in comparison with their experiences on board *Véronique*. Eustace preserved a List of Passengers; and here we find the Earl, the Admiral, Mr Durnford, Captain Bulkeley, Captain North, Mr Yarborough and Mr Smith, all in the First Class Saloon. In particular they enjoyed a sumptuous *Dîner d'Adieu* on 24 January 1905. The rest of those who had accompanied Fitzwilliam to Cocos Island, some 41 men in all, came home on board a steambucket called the *Trent*, where it is doubtful that they enjoyed much comfort, let alone luxury. They arrived in Plymouth on 8 February, 1905.[43]

Such are the facts relating to Earl Fitzwilliam's voyage and exploration of Cocos Island in the winter of 1904-5; but, as we shall see, the inhabitants of Grub Street were to tell a very different story, indeed several different stories, some of which bore little resemblance to the truth.

---

42 Doncaster Archives, DZ/MZ/30/Y1.

43 *Northampton Mercury*, 10 February 1905.

Chapter 5

RUMOURS AND SPIN

Speculation began to build as Fitzwilliam was steaming home from the Caribbean. On 7 January 1905 the *Sheffield Daily Telegraph* reported that

'Society has been perturbed this afternoon by the serious news which has come to hand at Lloyd's regarding Earl Fitzwilliam and his treasure hunting ship, the *Véronique*. It is of interest – with an added element of hope – that this was not the first time that news of a disaster to Earl Fitzwilliam has been circulated. The first occasion was about nine years ago, when his lordship (the Viscount Milton) was reported as having been killed in the hunting field in South Yorkshire. One can only hope that this second adventure will turn out to be as painless to himself as the first.'

There was something in the wind. What was this 'serious news'? The *Daily Express* pestered Cecil Cowper for more information, but he had none. The Earl had not cabled him, nor had he contacted the Countess Fitzwilliam, or her father, the Marquess of Zetland. The shipping correspondent for the *Daily Telegraph* could merely report that the Earl had set off from England the previous Autumn and that the *Véronique* had safely reached Montevideo in Uruguay on 30 November; but on 6 January a telegram had been received from Fitzwilliam containing only four words 'Accident. I am safe.

This was hardly going to put out the fire. The news had already produced a dramatic if temporary effect on the re-insurance rates for ships at Lloyd's, especially because another British vessel, the *Menantic*, had recently been lost in the South Pacific, and some said that the *Véronique* might have been wrecked on one of the many islands between the Straits of Magellan and Valparaiso.

The following day, 8 January, the *Yorkshire Evening Post* reported that its correspondent had called at the Earl's London home in Grosvenor Square not once but twice, and on the second occasion had been told of a second telegram received at Lloyds. 'Accident: everybody all right, returning home at once, arriving in England 26th. Slightly hurt but quite well again. Mr Bulkeley also cut about head.' A third telegram was then received in Sheffield by Stephen Smith, brother of David. 'Accident, your brother all right. Fitzwilliam.'

Commenting on the hike in the Lloyds' re-insurance rate, the *Post* reported that '45 guineas per cent were reported to have been paid on the vessel at Lloyd's during the day.' The 'vessel' referred to here was the *Véronique*, whereas we know now that the Earl was already homeward bound on another ship. The *Post* concluded by telling its readers that the Earl had left England on 21 November 1904, had travelled to his destination via Cape Horn, and had gone in search of coal. All these statements were inaccurate.

On 10 January *The Times* and *The Manchester Guardian* each reported that the Royal Mail Steampacket Company had received a telegram at its Southampton offices, from Captain Morrison of the *Véronique*, with news of a Southampton man called Hester who had been a waiter on board her.

'Hester, waiter, badly injured; landslide, Cocos; gone hospital; others all well – MORRISON.'

The Times went on to say that Earl Fitzwilliam had boarded *Orinoco* at Colon in Panama. She was due to reach England on the 26th. The same newspaper carried a later report that Fitzwilliam had reached Kingston, Jamaica and was now on his way home 'after an unsuccessful prospecting search for coal, an outcrop of which existed years ago on Cocos Island, west of Panama'. On Saturday 14

January 1905 the *Edinburgh Evening News* carried a story, said to derive from the *New York Herald*, that men from Harold Gray's yacht *Rose Marine* had landed on Cocos Island before Fitzwilliam's, and a fight had broken out between the two parties as soon as *Véronique* arrived. Gray's men had fought off Fitzwilliam's until the Costa Ricans sent a gunboat, *Turrialbia*, to restore law and order. A garbled version of the same story appeared in other newspapers, in which Fitzwilliam's men had been victorious.

On 16 January both *The Manchester Guardian* and the *Yorkshire Evening Post* returned to the fray. The *Post* carried the report of yet another telegram, sent by Earl Fitzwilliam to his secretary from Barbados, which instructed Cowper to 'contradict absurd rumours in press concerning supposed treasure hunting expedition.' The Earl had also given an interview in Barbados, in which he asserted that the object of his expedition had been to search for minerals, but that they had discovered coal. He specifically denied that he had been treasure-hunting, saying that the confusion must have arisen because there were currently three other expeditions in the Pacific, all of them looking for buried treasure. However, it was true that some members of the party had met with an accident, on 31 December. They had placed some charges of gelignite in the side of a cliff, and because of recent rainfall, this had triggered a landslide, in which three of his men were entombed. Further, a second landslide had buried the rescuing party, and several serious injuries had been sustained. The *Post* then expressed its gratitude to his Lordship for clarifying the position, while at the same time providing a story which was 'refreshing', compared to the prevailing public concern about 'the fiscal question and the unemployed.'[44]

Rumours continued to fly until Thursday 26 January 1905, when the *Orinoco* arrived back in Plymouth. *The Manchester Guardian* and the *Yorkshire Post and Leeds Intelligencer* now claimed that permission had been sought for a select group of pressmen to come on board the vessel, but this had been refused, and indeed R.M.S. had taken steps to prevent any would-be interviewers from even setting foot on the steamer. However, some London journalists had chartered a

---

44 There is also a very full account in the *Northampton Mercury*, 13 January 1905, which states that Fitzwilliam took a 'boring plant' and 'an analyst's laboratory' with him on the outward voyage. See also the *Tamworth Herald*, 14 January 1905.

tug, while others made their way into the Sound in a sailing boat. The *Sheffield Telegraph* reported that around 100 pressmen had taken to the water;[45] but no vessel was allowed to come alongside *Orinoco* and the Earl kept well out of sight, presumably hoping to prevent the Edwardian *paparazzi* from snapping him from afar. The situation was only redeemed, so far as the Press were concerned, because other members of the party came on deck and Admiral Palliser, whom the Earl had no power to command, 'moved about freely'. Moreover, the old man

'was overheard to speak of the accident with the stranger who boarded the vessel and it is understood that the gallant Admiral admitted having been treasure-hunting [but] after this his third attempt he will make no farther effort to recover the bullion which was deposited on the Cocos Islands in 1835.'

The journalist who wrote these words clearly thought that he had a scoop on his hands, though it is noticeable that he confused Cocos Island with the Cocos Islands. It is also clear from the same report that the pressmen continued to pester other people on board the *Orinoco*, apart from the Admiral. After all, *Orinoco* was a mail ship, and did not belong to Fitzwilliam, as *Véronique* had done. There were passengers on board, who might be able and willing to talk, though the Earl and *Orinoco*'s owners had requested them not to. At least one passenger did break ranks and said

'We have been pledged to secrecy. But, as a matter of fact, very little is known of the affair. It has not attracted very much attention on board among the passengers. All that we really know is that the Earl has been treasure-seeking, despite the repeated denials, and that the search has been abandoned as a result of the explosion. There is absolutely no truth in the story that the men were killed and injured in a fight with a rival search expedition.'

---

45 *Sheffield Telegraph* 27 January 1905.

If this was meant to dampen down the feeding-frenzy, it signally failed to do so. Speculation reached new heights on 27 January 1905, when reports appeared in several newspapers, including the *Manchester Courier*, the *Morning Post* and the *Standard*. Indeed the *Daily Telegraph* ran an even more extraordinary story under the heading

EARL FITZWILLIAM'S HEROISM
THRILLING INCIDENTS OF THE TREASURE SEARCH

'Lord Fitzwilliam, who was afloat in a boat, immediately jumped overboard, and swam onshore through the surf, to the total disregard of the sharks that infested the place. Under his direction, the hands were soon hard at work, extricating the buried men... Five bodies, consisting of Mr Bulkeley, Fowler, a miner; Bowles, a petty officer; a steward, and a negro workman, were laid out fearfully mangled. Lord Fitzwilliam had his head cut, and was smothered in blood from head to foot.'

Another paper even published a cartoon, lampooning the Earl and his friends.

THE CRUISE OF THE *VÉRONIQUE*
(WILL EARL FITZWILLIAM'S TREASURE-SEEKING START A NEW SOCIETY CRAZE?)

The cartoonist had drawn a belted Earl, an Admiral in full dress uniform, and several other 'toffs' and their wives, all busy surveying or digging on a tropical beach with palm trees, whilst a sailing ship rode at anchor in the bay.

The Earl still hoped to keep a lid on the whole affair; and so, by the time they reached Southampton, he had devised a cunning plan. David Smith picked up the Earl's despatch box and overcoat, pretended to be his valet and boarded the London express. The Press fell for it and boarded the same train. Fitzwilliam stayed a while longer on the *Orinoco* and then disembarked quietly, took breakfast with the Countess and caught a later train to London, where the couple stayed in their town house in Mayfair, before travelling home to Yorkshire.

The trick served only to raise the temperature. On the same day as the Earl arrived home *The Cornishman* published an article entitled

THE HUNT FOR PIRATES' TREASURE
EARL FITZWILLIAM'S MIRACULOUS ESCAPE

This was followed by a report from Jamaica, filed on 13 January, which stated that Fitzwilliam had been hunting for treasure, buried by the notorious Captain Morgan. This was complete invention, since Morgan lived between 1635 and 1688 and had been active in the Caribbean, not the Pacific. Interestingly, however, *The Cornishman* also reported that Fitzwilliam had sailed round the Horn; there had been at least two explosions; he had been severely injured and fourteen others were also hurt. Finally the Earl had been interviewed in Port of Spain, Trinidad on his way home, where he had stoutly maintained that he had never been treasure-hunting in his life. All this was highly inaccurate.

The general public was now being led to believe that Fitzwilliam was a fool and a knave; and that several of his men had been killed and several more severely wounded, on his watch. The Earl decided it was time to speak out. He gave an interview 'in order to settle for all time some of the 'mysterious' and 'miraculous' stories connected with his voyage to the South Pacific.' His secretary also issued a statement to a representative of the *St James's Gazette*.[46]

The Earl made his contempt for 'the gentlemen' of the Press' very clear. Much of what they had printed had been highly-coloured and exaggerated; they had behaved in a very shabby way; they had relied on hearsay and not even taken the trouble to verify what they printed. In fact, there had been no need to seek any further information, when all there was to know had been contained in the Earl's cables, already published in the newspapers. In addition the Press had been cruel and callous, because he had been inundated by anxious

---

46 *Sheffield Daily Telegraph*, 28 January 1905.

enquiries from relatives of men in his party, as to the welfare of their loved ones, prompted by the speculation.

The facts were simple, said Fitzwilliam. He had gone in search of minerals, not treasure; *Véronique* was a yacht, but not 'the largest yacht afloat'; he had not encountered any other treasure hunters whilst on Cocos Island; nobody had been killed there and only one labourer and Mr Yarborough had been injured; no-one had been 'completely buried'; the labourer was the only man whose injuries were serious; and even then he had not been 'smashed to a pulp'; and it was absolutely untrue that his own head had been 'swathed in bandages'. As for the story that he had swum through shark-infested waters when he heard the explosion, the Earl said 'I never swam a stroke from the day I left England to the day I came back'. His final words were 'the nearest approach I ever had to it was getting into a big bath.'

Chapter 6

A SECOND EXPEDITION?

The newspapers published much that was untrue; but Fitzwilliam had not done enough to scotch all the rumours. In particular, he had failed to give a convincing explanation as to why he had gone to Cocos Island in the first place. Before he left England, he had told the *Manchester Courier and Lancashire General Advertiser* that 'much coal' had been washed up on the beaches on the Island over time, and that he could see the local market for it expanding greatly once the Panama Canal was completed. After he got back he told the *Northampton Mercury* that

> 'The reports as to treasure hunting are all wrong. The object of the expedition was… to seek for minerals. That was why the engineer, Mr Durnford, and some expert miners, were among the party. The geological surveys were incorrect respecting the form of the minerals found in Central America. They had discovered coal, for example, where it was thought impossible that coal could exist.'[47]

---

47 *Manchester Courier* etc, 14 January 1905; *Northampton Mercury*, 20 January 1905. During an interview with the *New York Times* in 1907 Gissler disclosed that he had found a vein of hard coal on the Island, though he did not know whether it was anthracite or bituminous: Hancock & Weston, 306.

Sceptics might have thought that Fitzwilliam had little need to look for coal in the Pacific when he already owned so much of it in South Yorkshire; but, to be fair to his Lordship, the point of looking for coal in Central America would not have been to bring it home, but use it locally. There was a great need for a coaling station there, since there was none in British hands between the Falkland Islands and Canada. However, Cocos Island was volcanic in origin and much too young, geologically speaking, to have economic deposits of coal; and, if were ever to be used as a coaling station, the coal would have had to be brought from Australia. All this was well known at the time, and there was little point in the Earl pretending otherwise.

In any case, the Press was hardly likely to believe Fitzwilliam as to the central purpose of his mission, when his companion-in-chief was Admiral Palliser, a man already well known everywhere as a treasure-hunter. Moreover, Palliser had let the cat out of the bag when he talked to the Press on his return, as did Fitzwilliam's secretary Cecil Cowper. Cowper had said that he could not go beyond his master's statement, but had then proceeded to admit that one of the objects of the expedition had indeed been to look for treasure.

Palliser and Cowper were not the only ones to let the side down. Some of the passengers on board the *Orinoco* had already talked to the Press, and in the months that followed, some members of the crew gave further interviews. In February 1905, the *Sheffield Evening Telegraph* reported that

'Several of the crew... declared that they were searching for treasure when the explosion occurred, and were engaged in cutting a road through the mountains across the island.'

The representative of the *Daily News* representative saw the third officer, Mr F.W.Wilson, who said

"This much I will tell you. We are back, and we are glad. I can only add that Lord Fitzwilliam acted like an English gentleman all the way through, and so did the guests who were with him".

The newsman asked "But what about the others?"

"Ah! There you are asking what I'm not going to tell. Before we left the boat today, every man was solemnly sworn not to divulge anything that took place."

The reporter would not take 'no' for an answer. He suggested to the officer that Colonel Carter was the only one wounded and drew the reply

"Goodness! No, there were several others."

"And what about the opposing party?" Clearly, the journalist thought that there had been a fight of some kind on the Island; but Wilson replied

"I am going to keep my word, and say nothing whatever, but we all ought to have Victoria Crosses."

The *Daily Express* carried a different story. According to this, when they heard of Fitzwilliam's claim that he had merely been looking for coal, those on board the *Orinoco* roared with laughter; and Colonel Carter said

"We don't look like miners, do we? We visited Cocos Island… and what sporting man would not land and search for the fabled treasure? But we did not find it. I only wish we had."

A more sombre note was sounded by others, who wished to remain anonymous. One of these said

"The four men who are now in hospital in Panama were dreadfully injured and, though they are not likely to die, they will never be able to work again"[48]

_____

48 *Sheffield Evening Telegraph*, 9 February 1905.

Why did the Earl want to hush things up, despite the difficulty of doing so? One answer seems to be that he planned to go back to the Pacific, but so did others, and these were seen as competitors, who should on no account be given information which might prove useful to them. In February 1905, the story in the *Sheffield Evening Telegraph* was headed

EARL FITZWILLIAM AND COCOS ISLAND
IS ANOTHER TREASURE HUNT IN CONTEMPLATION?

'Captain Hackett, who commanded the last expedition in search of treasure in the Cocos Islands [sic] which started from Victoria, British Columbia, on the brigantine *Blakeley*, has reported a cablegram from Earl Fitzwilliam, asking him to come to England at once and offering to pay his expenses.'[49]

Over a year later, in March 1906, the *Dundee Courier* reported that an American, Mrs Roswell Hitchcock, would lead a fresh expedition to the Island

'In the hope of finding the supposed buried treasure which Lord Fitzwilliam's party recently tried to unearth. It is stated that Admiral Palliser, who accompanied Lord Fitzwilliam's party will be a member of the expedition, which will be financed by a Boston millionaire.'[50]

There was also a story in the *Dundee Evening Telegraph* on 6 August 1906, to the effect that Fitzwilliam was fitting out the steamship *Xema* for the purpose of another attempt. Large quantities of rifles, ammunition and dynamite were being sent to Cardiff, since dynamite was needed 'to blow up rocks on the island.' This was followed by several reports that

---

49 *Sheffield Evening Telegraph*, 16 February 1905.

50 *Dundee Courier*, 13 March 1906.

'the treasure-hunting steamer *Xema* has left Gravesend for a mystery port, popularly supposed to be Cocos Island where, as everyone knows, there is a vast store of pirates' loot. It is suspected that Lord Fitzwilliam is interested in the present venture. The crew have signed articles for St Helena, but this is merely due to the fact that the vessel will take in water, vegetables and coal there, and the Board of Trade requires a port of destination in the ship's articles. The present move in the direction of the pirates' hoard is quite sudden. It was thought that Earl Fitzwilliam had discarded [the *Xema*] for he found on the last expedition that she rolled horribly, and that her coal consumption for work done was terrific. Indeed, she got no further than the Bay when the expedition had to put back to Southlech Castle, renamed her *Véronique* and found Cocos Island in her, with results that are well known.' [51]

This is mostly nonsense. It was true that *Véronique* had been a 'roller'; but her original name was *Harlech Castle*, not *Xema*, and there is no evidence that she was subsequently renamed *Xema*, or that she ever returned from the Bay of Biscay for alterations.

In fact, it is most unlikely that Admiral Palliser took part in any further expedition, since he had announced after Fitzwilliam's expedition that he had given up treasure-hunting, and he died on 20 March 1907. [52] As for Fitzwilliam, there is no hard evidence that he was ever involved in another such venture, despite reports in the *Sheffield Evening Telegraph* and the *Yorkshire Telegraph and 'Star'*, on 25 May 1907, that he was.

---

51 *Hull Daily Mail*, 6 August 1906; *Lichfield Mercury*, 10 & 16 August 1906.

52 *Leeds Mercury* 21 March 1907. See also the report of Palliser's death in the *Yorkshire Telegraph and 'Star'*, 19 March 1907.

EARL FITZWILLIAM'S TREASURE HUNT
SECOND EXPEDITION COMES TO GRIEF

'A dispatch [sic] from New Orleans to the *Montreal Witness* reports the arrival there of the *Anselm*, having on board the crew of the steamship *Attiquin*, a private vessel belonging to the Earl Fitzwilliam... She cleared from Bristol, England, for Tampa and Belize, British Honduras, which point she left for a voyage around Cape Horn, her destination being Cocos Island, off the west coast of Central America, where it was the intention to search for treasure. The vessel was beached and wrecked, however, off the coast of Honduras, and is a complete loss. The crew, the correspondent says, narrowly escaped with their lives. This is the second expedition sent out by Earl Fitzwilliam within the past three years, to uncover the fabled treasure on Cocos Island, that has come to grief.'

The story of a second expedition also gained some purchase outside Yorkshire. On 25 December 1907 the *Aberdeen Journal* reported that Fitzwilliam was 'interested' in a voyage to be undertaken to Cocos Island by a Mr Claud Robert Grieves Robinson, said to have obtained the sole right to explore the island for two years. Whether this was true may be doubted, especially since the *Journal* appended an unlikely tale that Fitzwilliam had recently assisted Herr Guissler [sic] to return to Cocos, after he had been forced to leave for want of funds.

One reason why these stories are far-fetched is that Fitzwilliam had many other interests and hobbies, apart from treasure-hunting. In 1907 he had founded the *Sheffield-Simplex* car company and become Master of the Galway Hunt in Ireland, promising to provide new kennels, stables and a pack.[53] In 1908 he opened a new colliery near Wentworth, known as Elsecar Main;[54] and in 1909 he became Lord Mayor of Sheffield. However, the Press was not willing to let the story go. So, when Fitzwilliam was adopted as the Master of the Galway, the *Nottingham Evening Press* repeated that

---

53 *Nottingham Evening Post*, 12 February 1907.

54 Elsecar Main closed in 1984, the year of the last Miners' Strike.

'the Earl took part in the recent unfortunate treasure hunt on Cocos Island, chartering the Union Castle liner, *Harlech Castle*, and renaming her *Véronique*, for the purpose.'[55]

Likewise, the Cocos expedition was mentioned again in 1909, when the main story was that Fitzwilliam intended to sell his Higham Ferrers estates in Northamptonshire.[56]

In September 1910, when Fitzwilliam hosted a reception for the T.U.C. as Lord Mayor of Sheffield, the *Northampton Mercury* reported that he was 'one of the most interesting men in the peerage' because

'In 1904 he seems to have headed an expedition to the islands of the Pacific, and the outcome was a wild story of an encounter between the party and a rival band of treasure seekers on the Cocos Island. It was asserted that in 1835 a great treasure was landed on the island and hidden away in a cave but the Earl denied any definite plan of treasure seeking. The story of the encounter probably arose from the fact that during the blasting operations carried out by his mining party on the island the Earl sustained a nasty scalp wound.'[57]

The story of Fitzwilliam's involvement in the treasure hunt was re-cycled again in 1911, on the occasion of the festivities he hosted for his son and heir's christening. There was even a story that Fitzwilliam had supported Gissler's claim to Cocos Island in 1904-5![58] In 1912, when two women joined a British expedition to Cocos Island, the *West Briton and Cornwall Advertiser* reported that the two ladies in question, Mrs Barry Till and Miss Davis, had joined the steamer *Melmore* in Panama

55 *Nottingham Evening Post*, 12 February 1907.

56 *Western Times*, 30 July 1909.

57 *Northampton Mercury*, 16 September 1910.

58 *Dundee Evening Telegraph*, 14 February 1911; *Yorkshire Post and Leeds Intelligencer*, 6 December 1911.

'taking with them charts, drawings and papers which were made when they were on Cocos Island last year, when they are reported to have located the exact whereabouts of the cave where the treasure was concealed by pirates. It is in a quite different part of the island, which is only four miles across, from the scene of Earl Fitzwilliam's researches...' [59]

Fitzwilliam's expedition also featured in Ralph Delahaye Paine's *Book of Buried Treasure*, published in London in 1911, and noticed in the *Yorkshire Post and Leeds Intelligencer* on 6 December. Paine (1871-1925) was an American adventurer who became a journalist and popular author, before turning his hand to politics. He wrote much about ships and the sea, and was certainly prolific. His book about buried treasure purported to be a complete history of the subject in sixteen chapters, so it is difficult to see that he had much time to check his facts. The few pages he devoted to Fitzwilliam are certainly inaccurate, though his readers may not have realised this, in view of Fitzwilliam's refusal to set the record straight.

Paine included a photograph of a bearded man in Wafer Bay, and the caption tells us this was 'Christian Cruse, the hermit treasure-seeker of Cocos Island', when it is clearly August Gissler. He described Earl Fitzwilliam as 'a wealthy British naval officer', when he was in the Army, not the Navy. He told how the Earl 'found poor Gissler in a Costa Rican port, became interested in his claims, and promptly supported his claims', which is completely at variance with the known facts. Supposedly, Fitzwilliam used his influence to procure a renewal of Gissler's rights as governor of the Island. He took him on board his 'yacht' and returned him to Cocos! After landing there, the Earl's men started digging next door to the English party led by Arnold Gray.[60] The two teams used bad language towards each other, 'the one accusing the other of effacing its landmarks and playing hob with its clues.' Finally 'the climax was a pitched battle in which heads were broken and considerable blood spilt.'

---

59 *West Briton and Cornwall Advertiser*, 18 July 1912.

60 Real name Harold Gray: *Tamworth Herald*, 14 January 1905.

The most sensational story about Fitzwilliam was published in the *Daily Mirror* three years later, on 4 February 1914 – six months before the outbreak of the First World War. One of the subheadings was

AN ORGY OF SCANDAL

The context was one of those society divorces which early 20th century newspapers and their readers found so fascinating, along with murder trials. A divorce petition had been brought by a banker, Mr Leslie Melville, alleging that his wife had committed adultery with two men, of whom Fitzwilliam was one. This came to the attention of the magazine *Modern Society*, which was edited by Frank Harris (1856-1931), later to become notorious as the author of *My Life and Loves* (1922-27), a book which was banned as downright pornographic in several countries. Harris began by asking a question

> 'Is Lord Fitzwilliam an ill-used man or a sly dog? The final blow to the King and Queen's faith in human kind is the petition of Mr Leslie Melville. Lord Fitzwilliam, if guilty, must be a sly dog because at the time King George and Queen Mary were enjoying his hospitality at Wentworth Woodhouse and Lord Fitzwilliam had always been regarded as one of the 'untouchables' of the nobility. Mrs Leslie Melville is of course 'the lady in the case' but what a story Lady Fitzwilliam could tell anyway. The Marquis of Zetland, her father, has not been on visiting terms at Wentworth Woodhouse for a long time and I hear that Lady Fitzwilliam is broken-hearted at the trouble over the coming Leslie Melville divorce, as if Mr Leslie Melville is successful, it will mean also the parting of the ways at Wentworth Woodhouse.'

Fitzwilliam was outraged; and he may have been equally put out by a second article in the same magazine, entitled 'How Lord Fitzwilliam escaped the boredom of the biggest house in England.' This included the following paragraph

COCOS ISLAND TREASURE

'When war did not offer opportunities of freedom, Fitzwilliam knew how to make them. One of his smartest ideas was that trip on the *Véronique* to the Pacific in search of the 'Cocos Island Treasure.' That the story of the treasure is a trick of the romanticist's imagination is pretty well known, but it was good enough for Lord Fitzwilliam. Lady Fitzwilliam was of course quite confident that Lord Fitzwilliam would return with not less than a million pounds' worth of gold and coin. Dear little soul. However, Lord Fitzwilliam did not sail on the ship, but turned up months later in Panama, and eventually took the ship to Costa Rica. Where he had been in the meantime remains a mystery.'

This was simply untrue, but Fitzwilliam had never been able to curb the Press. He chose not to sue, and there was no Press Complaints Commission in 1914. However, he could and did decline to give interviews; and there is no record that he ever said anything to the Press about his expedition after 1905. It is also evident that he expected his servants, his employees and his friends to maintain a dignified silence. In the main, they did not let him down.

Chapter 7

THE CHEERIO TRAIL

In 1904-5 British society was aristocratic and deferential. Britannia ruled the waves and the British Empire occupied large swathes of the globe. Fitzwilliam inhabited a world fit for boys and men brought up on ripping yarns, with the money and the freedom to roam the oceans. It was also a world where the white man's word was law, and class distinctions at home were set in stone.

Many things changed during the First World War (1914-1918) and as a result of it. The British Empire became even larger on paper; but its economic and military strength had been holed below the waterline. In particular, coal had ceased to be the main driver of the British economy. The world's ships now ran on oil and there was no further use for coaling stations. Refrigeration and free trade had all but destroyed British agriculture. Now the Great War, the Great Crash and the Great Depression destroyed British supremacy in industry and commerce. In the 1920s the difficulty in getting servants was crippling the great families, or so they said.

Yet, for reasons no journalist was able to discern, nothing seemed to interfere with Fitzwilliam's way of life. Some members of his class sold off their mansions, some had them pulled down, others let them fall into ruin; but not Fitzwilliam. He had always been a 'big spender'. In 1902 he had paid for his entire staff to attend the Coronation of Edward VII; but what was remarkable was that he carried on spending, all through the bleak 1930s.

So it was that, in 1931, when his son and heir came of age, the Earl decreed that the occasion be celebrated in style. The 'Milton Committee', chaired by Captain North, decided that Lord Milton's birthday would be the culmination of a week's events, and that 15,000 people would be entertained in Wentworth Park. The task was made manageable by North's insistence that there be a strict segregation of classes. North ordained that there were seven of these; and invitations were duly issued to officials & heads of department; household staff; estate employees; colliery and chemical works employees; farm tenants; cottage and other tenants; and leaseholders. Classes 1, 2 and 3 would be permitted to mingle, as would classes 4 and 6; but not the others. There were to be six parties in total, including several balls. There would be a funfair in the Park for classes 3, 4 and 6; and a birthday ball later in the Marble Salon at Wentworth for classes 1 and 2. Class 7 might have a ball of its own.[61]

The public's interest in Cocos Island also survived the Great War. The journey from Britain was of course much shorter after the opening of the Panama Canal in 1914; but the Island continued to attract explorers from all over the western world.

In 1922 the *Sunday Post* reported that a Miss Jane Sands, daughter of an Englishman who was connected with the diplomatic service in Costa Rica, was about to set off for the Island. In 1924 the *Western Morning News* reported that Cocos Island had been included in the South Pacific programme of the Scientific Expeditionary Research Association, for which the yacht *St George* was currently being fitted out in Dartmouth. In the same year, a Canadian expedition, headed by a Captain Polkinghorne set off from Vancouver, in a 'little steamer' named *Gunner*. It was reported that Polkinghorne had already made two similar ventures in vain but was confident that he would find the treasure this time.[62]

In 1926 Sir Malcolm Campbell (1885 – 1948) took up the baton. People of our generation remember his son Donald, who was killed when his boat *Blue Bird* turned over on Coniston Water in the Lake District in 1967; but the father was more famous than the son in his day, setting 13 land and water speed records

---

61 Bailey, 288-9.

62 *Sunday Post* (Lanarkshire), 14 May 1922; *Western Morning News*, 1 September 1923, 24 January & 2 February 1924; *Yorkshire Evening Post*, 29 March 1924; *The Manchester Guardian*, 5 February 1924.

during the 1920s and 1930s. Sir Malcolm travelled to Cocos Island with Lee Guinness (1887 – 1937), a member of the Irish brewing family who had once held the world land speed record himself, and invented the spark plug. Guinness provided the yacht, suitably called *Adventuress*. Campbell wrote

'I visited Cocos Island in 1926 with a small party of friends who were not really enthusiastic over this treasure hunt, they all being too scep-tical and believed that the whole thing was a fairy story... I already had in my possession the clue to the *Mary Dear* treasure... My friends expected that they would come across the treasure five minutes after landing and, because we were not immediately successful, they lost heart. I lived on the island with two seamen in a tent for a matter of seventeen days, and we had to leave hurriedly.'[63]

Campbell refers to Fitzwilliam's expedition only once, when he describes the 'derelict broken down ruins of several huts' which he found in Wafer Bay.

'I believe these huts were occupied by Earl Fitzwilliam's party when he led his famous expedition to Cocos Island more than twenty years ago.'[64]

We know now that Campbell was quite wrong about this. The huts he found must have belonged to Gissler, whose settlement was in Wafer Bay, rather than Fitzwilliam, whose explorations were based on Chatham Bay.

A second Campbell-Guinness expedition to the Island was planned for 1931; but the *Hartlepool Mail* reported somewhat sardonically

'It is a pity there is no golf-course on Cocos Island. I do not think they will find much else to do there. The last time I was in Panama, a Cuban showed me a map of Cocos Island. He pointed to a cross on the map

---

63 *The Observer*, 12 January 2003; Hancock & Weston, 129-130, 141.
64 Campbell, 172,

at the foot of a hill. "Under that spot, Señor" he said impressively "Is buried gold, silver, and jewels worth £6,000,000". "Why hasn't anyone got it out?" I asked. "They didn't have the equipment" he said. Since then I have heard all over South America of the treasure of Cocos, which has been valued at £2,000,000, £4,000,000, £5,000,000 and £8,000,000. I have seen three other maps of the island. Scores of people have dug it up until it looked like a rabbit warren but all the treasure seems still to be there. It is now valued, I read last night, at £12,000,000. But they will have to hurry. For three weeks ago I met a man who was on the eve of sailing for the Island himself. He thinks there is only £8,000,000 there. If he gets there first, I hope there won't be a fight over all this wealth.' [65]

Instead of speculating on the total value of the treasure, other reporters dwelt on the fabulous nature of what remained to be found. According to one, there were 175 tons of silver dollars, a deep pit of gold-hilted swords, a golden triangle studded with jewels, and 'a crown whose midmost diamond is as large as a pigeon's egg'. According to another, the hoard included 300,000 pounds of silver and gold dollars, 733 bricks of gold, each 24 cubic inches, 273 gold-hilted swords, and 'several kettles filled with gold coin.'[66]

In the 1930s, the treasure hunters on Cocos Island were still capable of idealism and even heroism, but the phrase 'Cocos Island treasure' now entered the language, to indicate a windfall;[67] and corporate endeavour and modern science were also in evidence, along with stock-jobbing, false prospectuses and plain skulduggery.

In 1932 Commander J. Plumpton, of Cullompton in Devon, organised an expedition with eight friends, who each made a financial contribution. These included Stratford Jolly and Frank Cooper, who had a glove-making business in Yeovil, but was also known as an all-purpose mechanic and metal diviner.

---

65 *Hartlepool Mail*, 20 November 1931.

66 *Aberdeen Journal*, 25 December 1907; *Yorkshire Post and Leeds Intelligencer*, 6 December 1911; *Nottingham Evening Post*, 6 July 1932.

67 *Dundee Courier*, 26 November 1931.

Another friend donated an old sailing ship, the *Vigilant*, which had been used as a trawler in Brixham. Plumpton (who contributed a mere £90) was determined to break new ground. He would not rely on old-fashioned methods. Instead he would rely on Frank Cooper, who supposedly had an uncanny ability to detect precious metal with a spring extracted from an old gramophone.[68]

When Plumpton arrived on Cocos Island, he found that a party of Canadians had forestalled him; and they had brought a small aeroplane and a new detecting device with them. This was the 'Metalophone', developed by W.H.Clayton of the Canadian Clayton Metalophone Company, whose promoters included Colonel J.E. Leckie, Captain C.A. Arthur (whom we shall meet again) and Stratford Jolly (one of Plumpton's so-called 'friends.').[69] The Metalophone resembled a primitive Geiger-Counter, and was extremely cumbersome and difficult to use anywhere. After some hesitation, the two parties agreed to join forces and spent some weeks searching for the treasure; but the Metalophone proved useless on Cocos Island, with its steep slopes and dense vegetation.[70]

Plumpton's own account of his adventures, in his book *Treasure Cruise* (published and reviewed in *The Manchester Guardian*)[71] does not tells us the whole story, by any means. Above all, it fails to make clear that the author experienced financial difficulties from the beginning; and the agreement with Clayton Metalophone did not put an end to them. Plumpton returned to England in 1932.

Although Commander Plumpton never claimed to have found any treasure on Cocos Island, there were reports in the *Nottingham Evening Post* and in the *Yorkshire Post and Leeds Intelligencer* on 23 June 1932, that pirate treasure 'optimistically believed to be worth £12,000,000' had been found, by Colonel Leckie – one of those involved in the Canadian company; and supposedly, the find had been made with an 'electrical diviner'. Then, on 6 July the *Dundee Courier* proudly announced that the Island, which had for generations 'exercised

---

68 Hancock& Weston, 148-9; *Western Times*, 2 June 1939. For Cooper's all round usefulness, see Plumpton, 189.

69 Hancock & Weston, Chapter 15.

70 Plumpton, 29, Chapter VI. The nature of the Metalophone is described in detail in Chapter VII.

71 *The Manchester Guardian*, 4 March 1935.

an irresistible spell for adventurous men' had at last yielded up its secret, to two Scotsmen no less, or at least to men of Scots origin.

CENTURY OLD SECRET HOARDS FOUND

Supposedly Leckie and Clayton had found the treasure, or some of it, some 30 feet from where Campbell and Guinness had looked for it only a few years before. The story was briefly referred to in the *Nottingham Evening Post* the same day. Unfortunately, there was never any confirmation of the find. It is certainly not referred to in Plumpton's book, and the probability must be that, if anything was discovered, it was fool's gold rather than the genuine article.

Clayton Metalophone seems to have ceased trading early in 1933; but Leckie was one of the backers of a new company formed in Britain in March 1934 by Captain Arthur. This was Treasure Recovery Ltd., and it was floated on the Stock Exchange, with the aim of raising £75,000. The company's prospectus boasted that the presence of treasure on Cocos was 'well-established by official government sources'. (There was no claim that any treasure had actually been discovered). The expedition would be launched in April and would arrive on the Island in May.[72]

In the event the new company mounted two expeditions. The first was undertaken on board the *Queen of Scots*, which left England in August 1934 and arrived in Wafer Bay on 26 September. The yacht was provided by a Mr Anthony Drexel junior.[73] Before setting off Captain Arthur claimed, like Plumpton before him, that he would use modern scientific methods: an aeroplane for surveying, electrical instruments for exploration, telephones for communication and the latest core-drills for digging.[74] The treasure awaiting discovery was now estimated to be worth between £12,000,000 and £25,000,000 and Captain Arthur claimed that he knew exactly where it was; but it was a feature of this voyage that he did not even bother to ask the Costa Ricans for permission to

---

72 Hancock & Weston, 155 & 313-6. Plumpton was aware of this venture: *Treasure Cruise*, 172.

73 Possibly the son of the American tycoon of the same name (1826-1893).

74 Hancock & Weston, 163; *Hartlepool Mail*, 20 August 1934.

land. Instead, he laid claim to the Island in the name of the British Crown, and hoisted the Union Jack as soon as he arrived.

The expedition was aborted when the chief engineer cracked his skull accidentally, had to be evacuated to Panama and died there. Captain Arthur wanted to continue, especially since he had left most of his crew on the Island; but the diplomatic chickens now came home to roost. The Panama Canal authorities impounded his ship for non-payment of tolls and duties, and the Costa Rican government barred the Captain from returning to the Island. His Majesty's Government was asked to intervene on his behalf, but declined to do so. The Costa Ricans sent two launches and 75 soldiers, who were lost at sea for a few days, but eventually arrived on Cocos, where they arrested 18 treasure hunters and confiscated all their equipment. Hearing of this, Drexel asked for the return of his yacht.

At this point, Captain Arthur abandoned his ship and his men and scuttled off back to England; but it is pleasant to report that his crew were all acquitted of any wrongdoing, since the Judge who heard the case thought that they had all been duped by their Captain.[75] 200 electric lamps which had been left on the Island were confiscated by the Costa Ricans and given to the penal colony on St Luke's Island, where members of Fitzwilliam's party had been so royally entertained in 1904. Arthur's crew were allowed to sail home on the *Queen of Scots*, returning to English shores at the end of November 1934.

Following this incident, it was reported that the Costa Rican government was going to establish a garrison, or perhaps a penal colony, on Cocos Island. Foreigners would be kept out and no-one would ever again be allowed to exploit the Island's potential riches; but in the event, the Costa Ricans did little more than issue postage stamps, to let the world know that the Island belonged to them.[76]

Captain Arthur was not a man who was easily embarrassed and, amazingly, he managed to restore relations with various members of the 1934 expedition. He persuaded them that there had been a 'misunderstanding' with the Costa

---

75 Hancock & Weston, Chapter 17.

76 *Western Morning News*, 20 December 1934; *Sunderland Daily Echo and Shipping Gazette*, 9 October 1934; *Yorkshire Post & Leeds Intelligencer*, 20 December 1934; *The Observer*, 10 November 1935 (stamps).

Ricans, but said that all would now be well, because he had done a deal with Clayton Metalophone and bought out its concession.

New capital was raised, for a second expedition in 1935. Another ship was acquired, called the *Veracity* (an odd name in the circumstances). She set sail for Cocos Island on 11 February, albeit without Captain Arthur. She reached Barbados on 23 April and Cocos Island on 9 June; but not everyone was content with these developments. In particular, some of Treasure Recovery's creditors petitioned the High Court in London to have the company wound up. Others took action against Captain Arthur personally and he was eventually made bankrupt, in 1939. The assistant Official Receiver informed the creditors' meeting that Arthur could not be found, because he was in Trinidad, fishing.[77]

The reader will not be surprised to learn that Treasure Recovery Ltd collapsed early in 1936, having used up all the shareholders' money, and leaving 1,500 creditors in the lurch; but, four years after publishing his book the intrepid Commander Plumpton returned to the fray, undaunted by his previous failure. Once again, he took Frank Cooper of Yeovil with him. Their destination was kept secret, though the newspapers speculated that Plumpton's aim was to find a sunken Spanish galleon, full of gold bullion and silver cannons. This time, they ran out of luck rather than money. Their ship *France* foundered in a storm some 33 miles off the coast of Guiana. Plumpton was found, after he had drifted for four days on the wreckage; but Frank Cooper never was.

The 1930s were therefore the heyday of treasure-hunting on Cocos Island; but interest in Fitzwilliam's expedition of 1904-5 had now begun to wane. It had been mentioned by Ralph Paine in 1911; but it did not feature in Plumpton's book in 1935. Nor does it appear in Hancock & Weston's history of treasure hunting on Cocos Island (1960), or in Hodge's later work on the same subject (2013).[78]

Fitzwilliam's name continued to appear in the newspapers but journalists found other things to write about him and his family. In the early 1930s, there were articles about one of his gamekeepers, who had been charged with shooting and killing an unemployed man in a wood known as Denaby Thick, but

---

77 *The Manchester Guardian*, 25 March 1939.

78 Hancock & Weston, 128-9; Hodge 237, 303-7.

who was discharged by the magistrates; about an outbreak of typhoid in Denby Dale and the Earl's provision of financial and other assistance; and about the marriage of Lord Milton to Lady Olive Plunket. In addition the family featured frequently in 'Court and Society' columns, for example when they attended the running of the St Leger in Doncaster in September 1937 and Lady Milton wore her furs.[79]

The Earl's treasure-hunting days were now a matter of minor importance so far as the Press was concerned; and in South Yorkshire, where his influence was still strong, they also remained mysterious. This was because the miners who sailed with Fitzwilliam to the far side of the world kept their word of honour and refused to talk about their experiences. So it was that the expedition of 1904-5 got its local name. As related by Roy Young in *Big House, Little Village* (2000, 2011) the story told in Wentworth in the middle years of the 20th century was that

> 'Those who took part in the journey of the *Véronique* held their peace and avoided giving an answer to questions as to their activities, generally by recalling an urgent appointment and so, 'Cheerio for now, I'll tell you about it some other time' – hence "The Cheerio Trip".'

With the substitution of 'trail' for 'trip', this was the story we both heard in Wentworth, forty or so years ago; and it told us next to nothing about what had actually happened in 1904-5. Yet the true story had been written years before, by the Earl's closest friends.

---

79 *The Manchester Guardian*, 26 March 1932; 7 September 1932; 9 November1932; 19 April 1933; *The Observer*, 12 September 1937.

Chapter 8

THE MYSTERY SOLVED?

avid Smith became a stockbroker, married and lived for a time at Hoober House, Wentworth; but he retired early in 1926.[80] He took up an interest in local history, becoming a founder member of the Hunter Archaeological Society and a regular contributor to various periodicals, including *Blackwood's Magazine*. In December 1932, he used this as a vehicle for an account of the great adventure of his youth, entitled *El Dorado*. Although he took care to anonymise the names of his fellow adventurers, there may well have been a breach of faith here; but we do not know whether Fitzwilliam treated it as such.

The article came to the attention of the *Nottingham Evening Post*, which ran a story entitled

BUCCANEERS OF 1904
ADVENTUROUS EXPEDITION IN
SEARCH OF PIRATES' HOARD. [81]

The Post said that Smith's description of the scene on Cocos Island after the miners had blown themselves up was reminiscent of some of the episodes in the Great War!

---

80 Obituary, THAS, volume VIII, part two, 1960, pp 105-6. This volume also has an incomplete article by Smith about his family: *The Smiths of Yorkshire and Glen Sherr.*
81 *Nottingham Evening Post*, 9 December 1932.

However, the fact was that *Blackwood's Magazine* was a relatively obscure publication, with a small circulation; and Smith's account was of little interest, compared to Sir Malcolm Campbell's book about Cocos Island, *My Greatest Adventure*, which had been published the previous year. Sir Malcolm was one of the most famous men of his day, and he publicised his book about Cocos Island on radio and by writing a preface to a history of treasure hunting in general, by Harold T. Wilkins, a British journalist who published several works on the subject.[82] Meanwhile, the secrets of the Cheerio Trail were kept safe, at least by Fitzwilliam's staff and employees.

David Smith was not the only one who wrote about the expedition of 1904-5. We now know that Eustace Cooke-Yarborough did too, at greater length, and contemporaneously. It is his Journal which forms the corner stone of this book; but Eustace chose to file it with his family papers once he had completed it; and his later life was a busy one. He succeeded to his family's Campsmount estate in 1915, was made Justice of the Peace in 1918, and became Chairman of the Doncaster Bench in 1923 and Chairman of West Riding Quarter Sessions in 1937. He died in 1938 without ever publishing his account of what he called *The Voyage of the Veronique R.Y.S. to the Pacific Ocean and After.*[83]

Cocos Island is now a National Park and a World Heritage Site and the only people allowed to live there are Costa Rican Park Rangers. The oceanographer Jacques Cousteau (1910-97) visited the seas around the Island several times, calling it the most beautiful in the world. So remote and unspoilt is it now that it has even been suggested as a source of inspiration for Michael Crichton's *Jurassic Park* (1993). Yet there were probably around 300 expeditions to the Island between 1870 and 1978. In this book we have been concerned mainly with British endeavours but there were probably as many American ventures as British,[84] while the bibliography compiled by the Cocos Island Research Centre suggests that the Germans were also very active.[85]

---

82 *The Manchester Guardian*, 11 January 1930 gave details of his radio broadcast. *Treasure Hunting* was published by Ivor Nicholson & Watson in London in 1932.

83 R.Y.S. stands for Royal Yacht Squadron, which seems inappropriate. Obituary in *Yorkshire Post and Leeds Intelligencer*, Friday 13 May 1938.

84 Plumpton, 13; Hodge, 4, 245, 260.

85 See www.oocities.org/thetropics.

Fitzwilliam's enterprise of 1904-5 was therefore by no means unusual; but, unlike some, the Earl paid for the entire operation himself, and raised no money from the public. He did not defraud anyone or issue dubious prospectuses. His ship was never impounded. He did his best to obtain the requisite permissions, or thought that he did; and he brought his men home in one piece, despite a degree of bad luck. He found nothing, but he was certainly not alone in that.

Fitzwilliam died in 1943 and was buried in the family graveyard behind the parish church in Wentworth village. Although forty years had passed since the expedition of 1904-5, at least one obituary writer still felt obliged to mention it.

'[The Earl] took part in an unsuccessful treasure hunt in the Cocos Islands, and was nearly killed during blasting operations.'[86]

Fitzwilliam's son and heir, the 8th Earl, was killed in a mysterious air crash in 1948, while the 9th Earl died in 1952. The estate therefore had to pay three sets of death duties, in less than ten years. The mines were nationalised in the 1940s and Fitzwilliam's wealth and influence was greatly diminished as a result.

Wentworth Woodhouse was leased out to Rotherham Council and from 1949 to 1976 it was a College of Physical Education, named after the 7th Earl's social-ist sister, Lady Mabel Smith. Later, it was used as halls of residence for Sheffield Polytechnic. Most of the contents were dispersed in auction sales. The Earldom became extinct in 1979, when the 10th Earl died. The mansion was sold to Wensley Haydon-Baillie in 1988 and to Clifford Newbold in 1999 and is currently for sale once more. Threatened by the costs of repair, its future remains uncertain.

Fitzwilliam never spoke about his expedition to Cocos Island after 1906 and, while he lived, he managed to impose a code of silence in Wentworth and the surrounding villages, which lasted into the 1950s and 60s. Why did he do this? Did he feel guilty about the expedition, or some aspect of it? Or was there something more to hide, some aspect of the adventure which was unknown even to Smith and Cooke-Yarborough, or which they knew about but chose not to divulge in their written accounts?

---

86 *Yorkshire Evening Post*, 15 February 1943.

David Smith's article of 1932 contains a coda, which does not feature in Eustace Cooke-Yarborough's journal but which is confirmed in an article in the *Nottingham Evening Post* for 9 December 1932. Supposedly, Fitzwilliam was summoned to Buckingham Palace when he returned from Cocos.

> 'Diplomatic trouble followed, and the leader of the band was "carpeted" by King Edward and duly admonished. That was not the finale, however, for, the castigation administered, the King rose from his chair and said to the culprit
>
> "You know perfectly well you ought not to have done it, but – by God, I wish I had been with you!"'

This is the first we have heard of any 'diplomatic trouble' in 1905, but it would not be surprising if there had been some concern in official circles about the Earl's activities. There was at least some doubt about the validity of his permit to excavate; and this may have caused him some embarrassment, in addition to the casualties which his men sustained whilst on Cocos Island, as a result of someone's incompetence with explosives.

Finally, there is an intriguing passage in Sir Malcolm Campbell's account of the seventeen days he spent on Cocos Island in 1926, which we have not yet quoted.

> 'I have heard rumours… that the treasure was removed thirty years ago from its original hiding place and secreted elsewhere. This may or may not be true…. I had a most interesting letter from another correspondent abroad, who states that he himself has been to Cocos, unearthed half the treasure and upon returning for the remainder some years later, was nearly engulfed in a landslide, and was unable to enter the cave in consequence.'

Now it is very unlikely that this anonymous 'correspondent' of Campbell's was Fitzwilliam; but let us suppose, for a moment, that it was. Then the Earl would really have had something to be secretive about for all those years; and the mystery of the Cheerio Trail would remain unsolved to this day.

SOURCES

Primary

The Cruise of the Véronique R.Y.S. to the Pacific and After 1904, journal and press cuttings by G Cooke-Yarborough: Doncaster Archives, The Cooke-Yarborough Collection DZ/MZ/30/Y1.

The British Newspaper Archive, www.britishnewspaperarchive.co.uk.

The Guardian & *Observer* Newspaper digital archive.

Transactions of the Hunter Archaeological Society (THAS).

Secondary

Bailey, Catherine, *Black Diamonds* (Penguin, 2007)

Campbell, Sir Malcolm, *My Greatest Adventure* (Butterworths, 1931)

Hancock, Ralph and Julian A. Weston, *The Lost Treasure of Cocos Island*, (Thomas Nelson & Sons, New York, 1960)

Hodge, John Samuel, *Treasures of Cocos Island* (John Samuel Hodge, 2013)

Jones, Melvyn, *Earl Fitzwilliam's Travels to Treasure Island* (unpublished typescript)

Viscount Milton & W.B.Cheadle, *The North-West Passage by Land* (Cassell, Petter and Galpin, London, 1865.

De Montmorency, Hervey, *On the Track of A Treasure, The Story of an Adventurous Expedition to the Pacific Island of Cocos in Search of Treasure of Untold Value Hidden by Pirates* (Hurst & Blackett, London, 1904)

Paine, Ralph D., *The Book of Buried Treasure* (W.Heinemann, London, 1911)

Plumpton, Commander James, *Treasure Cruise, The Voyage of the* Vigilant *to Cocos Island* (H.F.&G.Witherby, London, 1935)

Smith, David T., *El Dorado*, (*Blackwood's Magazine* December 1932 pp 843-850)

Young, Roy, *The Big House and the Little Village* (Wentworth Garden Centre, 3rd edition, 2011)

ILLUSTRATIONS

Cocos Island Map

Wentworth Woodhouse, 2014

Earl Fitzwilliam's House in London, 2014

The 7th Earl Fitzwilliam

Admiral Palliser

The Véronique

St Vincent's Harbour

The little dog & the ship's cat

Bulkeley washing dog

Bulkeley & cow

Eustace at rest

Captain North, Captain Morrison, Admiral Palliser

St John Durnford in Montevideo

Smythe's Channel, the Véronique at anchor

Old building in Panama

Brooke and his Panama family

Bulkeley

Native ox wagon, Puntarenas

View from St Luke's Island, Costa Rica

Hunting party on St Luke's Island

Hunting the shark

Fitzwilliam en route to San José

Cocos Island

Chatham Bay

The cow on Cocos Island

The British camp in Chatham Bay

The main tent in Chatham Bay

Bulkeley, Fitzwilliam & Gissler, Chatham Bay

Gissler in the German settlement, Wafer Bay

R.M.S. Orinoco

R.M.S. Trent

Constant Springs Hotel, Jamaica

Street vendors in Barbados

Brooke in Barbados

The Dîner d'Adieu

Cartoon, 1905

Made in the USA
Columbia, SC
27 August 2018